AGATHA'S JOURNEY
1828 - 1998

AGATHA'S
JOURNEY
1828 - 1998

SANDRA PENROSE

**Custom Sensor Solutions Inc.,
Naperville, Illinois, USA**

Custom Sensor Solutions, Inc.
526 West Franklin Avenue
Naperville, IL 60540
Email: info@customsensorsolutions.com
Web: www.customsensorsolutions.com/books.htm

Created by William and Sandra Penrose.
Printed and bound by United Graphics, Inc., Mattoon, IL
Cover design by Vickie Swisher, Studio 20/20, Toledo, IL

Author and publisher have taken care to report the facts of this story as correctly and realistically as possible. However, in some cases, names and circumstances have been altered to protect the identities of certain persons.

ISBN 0-9664590-0-8
Library of Congress Catalog No. 98-93181

This book is dedicated to my husband, Bill,
and to my parents, Howard and Dorothy Bulbrook.

Foreword

by Lynnea Andolfi, N.D., Ph.D.

As a psychologist, naturopathic physician, and psychic, I am intimately concerned with the connections among mind, body, and spirit. Agatha's tale explores those connections. We are all aware of the powerful effect that emotions and attitude can have on our health. Many people have been known to prolong life, spontaneously cure themselves of incurable diseases, and survive against hopeless odds by sheer force of will. We do not yet know whether, or how, these same powerful forces can act beyond the curtain of death. Agatha's experience, as related to Sandra Penrose, suggests that they can. Even when finally overcome by her lonely battle with the elements, Agatha persists among us so that her tale can be told.

Agatha's Journey forces us to remember that we must keep the three parts of life -- mind, body, and spirit -- in balance. For Agatha, the driving force was her obsession, first to see her daughter's grave consecrated, and ultimately to see that her tale was told. This single-minded obsession allowed her physical body to survive in the wilderness under impossible conditions, but at the same time, it prevented her from seeking help from the growing settlement nearby. After her inevitable death, the same fixation kept her anchored to the earth. Whether we are appalled by her failure to seek help, or empathize with her depression and isolation, such is the nature of obsession.

Agatha's Journey can be read from many perspectives. It is an historically wonderful tale. It is also a tragic love story, with a strong heroine. Primarily, however, it is about the courageous spirit residing in all of us, that is able to transcend time and space. Together, Sandra and Agatha underscore once more the truth that, as human beings, we are capable of accomplishing anything we choose. But most of all, the story of Agatha's tragic life beautifully encapsulates the human drama: loving, losing, forgiving, and finally, letting go.

Preface

When Pat Williams suggested that I write Agatha's story, I had no idea what a project it would become. The 1830s on the American Frontier were an unexpectedly difficult period to research. The first settlers were too busy clearing land and building, and few records were kept. When written histories began to appear in the 1840s and '50s, the authors had to depend mainly on second- and third-hand stories. Until now, Agatha Wilson was just one of the anonymous multitude of early pioneers who vanished into the American wilderness.

Agatha gave me few details about her friendship with the Potawatomi, although it was crucial to her survival. For simplicity's sake, I have used the name of Shattee, a Potawatomi chief who helped evacuate the settlers during the Black Hawk war, to represent all the Potawatomi who helped Agatha. The recipe for cornmeal mush was derived from *Wagon Wheel Kitchens*, by Jacqueline Williams (University Press of Kansas, 1993). The stories of bravery and cowardice during the 1832 Black Hawk war were found in several history books, but none so colorful as *"That Disgraceful Affair", the Black Hawk War*, by Cecil Eby (W. W. Norton & Co., 1973).

Kathy Fitch, a Professor of English at the College of DuPage, spent a great deal of time helping to edit this book. She convinced me to include more personal details to describe the effect the spirits had on my family. Kathy also had some valuable suggestions for the cover. But most of all, her constant encouragement enabled me to finish the revisions so the book could be published.

The following people provided helpful comments as the writing evolved:

> Dr. Lynnea Andolfi
> Frank Asta
> Maureen Berk
> Kathy Heroux
> Bill Penrose
> Howard and Kathy Penrose
> Roger and Jennifer Penrose
> Ron and Marilyn Pumphrey
> Heather Ramsey
> Debby Ryel
> Sue Vecero
> Pat Williams

I appreciate the cooperation of the staff at the Naper Settlement who made pertinent information in their library available to me. I also made much use of the Local History resource at The Nichols Library of Naperville, and the Township of Naperville Assessor's Office, where I was allowed me to inspect the old maps to verify details of early Naperville.

Information about the history of the Naperville area was provided by the following people:

> Judy Fessler
> Alma Miller
> Jonelle Nuttal
> John Shimp
> Joe Weigand

SECTION 1

DISCOVERING AGATHA

Prolog

I'm alone in the house, sitting in the living room, becoming more and more terrified. The anger in the house is building up again. I watch the back stairs, just off the kitchen, expecting at any moment to see his head appear above the back counter as he reaches the top of the stairs. He? It? What is there in the basement that has me so terrified? I'm afraid it will come up into the kitchen. It never has before; maybe it can't. It's as if some force were keeping it confined to the basement. But the atmosphere of malevolence is growing stronger, and I wonder how much longer it can be contained.

I try to look away from the kitchen, but the feeling that it will soon reach the top of the stairs, that it wants to chase me out of the house, is overwhelming. Oh, why doesn't somebody come home! I look at the clock. It's only 7:30. No one else is due back for at least another hour. Outside it's a dark and cold October night; inside, the feeling of foreboding has been building up to something palpable. It has reached the kitchen and is approaching the dining room. Soon it will reach the living room...

"This is foolish!" I tell myself. "There's no one here but me and my overactive imagination." I will myself to get up and walk over to the stereo. "I'll put on some music," I say, thinking the music will distract me and take away this terror. My heart is pounding as I reach into the cabinet to select a record album. The ominous feeling grows, until I sense that danger is only a few steps away. Grabbing just any album, I begin to remove it from the record jacket. I no longer care what the music is. Anything to drown out this feeling of...

3

"Get out!" a male voice says inside my head. It's a voice full of venom. The tone is menacing; it's more of a whispered threat, not a shout. Instinctively I turn and look towards the kitchen. No one is there. No one is in the room with me, and yet I heard him.

I drop the album and hurry to the front door. It's a cold night and I have on only jeans and a sweater. I throw open the main door and stare out through the storm door window at the quiet street, trying to convince myself that this can't possibly be happening. The voice doesn't speak again, but menace hangs in the air. I feel a presence coming down the stairway from the second floor. Although I don't hear any footsteps on the stairs, something is pressuring me to leave for my own sake. I'm surrounded.

If I'd been upstairs in my bedroom when this whole thing started, I'd be safe right now. For some reason, this sinister atmosphere can't make it past the window seat on the second floor. This thing could not have reached me from the basement. I would have been protected by... by what? By something I can't see in the window seat? It somehow guards the upstairs, but now I don't dare try to go up there. I can't fight against this added pressure to get out of the house. Its force is growing stronger, more urgent. I throw open the storm door and escape onto the porch.

It's cold outside, too cold for the sweater I'm wearing, but I can't bring myself to go back in for a jacket. I sit down on the steps and hug myself for warmth. There's no car in the driveway to take me away from here. Bill has it. I don't know the neighbors well enough to pretend I'm dropping by for a social visit. I'm stuck here, growing colder by the minute.

I feel foolish and I'm shivering, but not enough to go back inside the house. That will take a while.

Chapter 1

In March of 1980, Bill and I moved into our current home with our children, Howard, 13, Roger, 11, and Heather, 8. From the day we moved in, I've loved our house. Built in the 1920's, it was originally a small, two-bedroom house with very little storage space. One of the previous owners expanded the dormers to add a full second floor, finished the basement, and built in storage everywhere. Although the house had been extensively renovated, nothing was done to destroy the character of the original design. When we moved in, we discovered that the house was full of unexpected nooks and crannies; later we realized that it was also full of spirits.

One of the spirits, undetected by us at first, was that of a forty-nine-year-old pioneer from the 1800s with a sad story to tell and an obsession to tell it. Her name was Agatha Wilson. Before we could hear her tale, however, we had to acknowledge that our family was not alone in the house. We then had to learn to remove some of the more insistent, and sometimes malevolent, spirits who had commanded all of our attention.

Soon after we moved in, I began to feel inexplicably unwelcome at certain times in some parts of the house. The atmosphere was similar to the feelings I would get when entering a home where a terrible argument had just happened; no matter how friendly the hosts might be, the anger hung in the air. Now, in my house, there were times when the air in some rooms seemed to be unpleasantly, electrically charged, as though such a violent argument had just occurred. This feeling would continue to build up until it was almost intolerable, but it never happened in our bedroom; I always felt safe there.

The unpleasant atmosphere could develop at any time of the day or night. Since we were new to the area and our children were at school, I was alone during the day, doing housework or reading. Because of the large size and sturdy construction of the house, the house was essentially sound-proof between floors. We had to install intercoms so that we could talk to each other between floors; shouting wasn't enough. As time went on, inexplicable noises combined with the oppressive atmosphere to further unnerve me. Sometimes, I would hear the sound of footsteps and of doors slamming on the second floor when I was on the main floor. I investigated thoroughly, at first, looking for some logical explanation for the noise, but found none. Eventually, I decided to get a pet so that another breathing creature was in the house with me.

In the summer of 1980, we got a dog from the Anti-Cruelty Society. Knight, a bizarre cross between a Labrador Retriever and a Dachshund, was quite hyperactive, much to my relief. There would be many times I could rationalize that the noises I heard must have come from this dog who was constantly on the go.

With Knight in the house for companionship, I began to relax. That was when I became aware of a presence on the second floor. There were three bedrooms and a bathroom up there. Bill and I had taken the smallest bedroom for ourselves and used the room attached to it as a dressing/sewing room. Heather occupied the larger front bedroom. I'd always found peace and comfort in our bedroom, even though I'd gradually developed the impression that there was a presence there of an old woman who had once lived in

6

the house. I hadn't seen anything to make me believe in her existence; it was just an impression that formed in my mind, like a story being told to me. Her existence was reassuring rather than disturbing. Not knowing what my family would think of my feelings in the house, I kept my fears and impressions to myself. I believed that our bedroom spirit liked to have us in the house. Her acceptance did not extend to everyone, however.

Once, when my parents were visiting, my mother went up to the bathroom on the second floor. Each upstairs bedroom has two doors, one leading to the front hall, and one leading to the back hall and the bathroom Mom had a choice of going through our room or our daughter's. She was about to go through our room when she got a strange feeling of foreboding and chose to go through Heather's instead. Our bedroom door closest to the bathroom was wide open when Mother passed it. When she came out again, she decided she had been silly to be afraid, and just to prove the point, started to go into our room. Again a nameless fear overtook her and she retraced her steps through our daughter's room to the front hall. As she reached the hall, she turned back and watched as our far bedroom door slammed shut. There had been no draft to cause this to happen. She hurried down the stairs. When we were alone, she told me about that day's events and a past problem she'd had.

"There's something wrong upstairs," she insisted. "Remember the last time I visited you and stayed in Heather's room by myself? One night, I heard a really loud thud coming from the closet, like a heavy box had dropped. I thought it would wake everybody up, but nobody else was disturbed, not even the dog. When I checked, there was nothing anywhere in the closet to make that noise. I hardly slept for the rest of the visit."

"That's odd. I always feel very comfortable upstairs," I said, though I was truly relieved that someone else found the house unsettling. But I did know what she meant. I had felt very unwelcome, not to mention terrified at times, in other parts of the house. I just didn't know how to talk about it.

Our daughter was as uncomfortable upstairs as my mother. Heather seldom had friends stay over, and when she did, she would usually ask if they could "camp out" on the living room floor with her. When we first moved in, Heather was afraid to go to bed at night. She would cry and tell us that she was frightened, but she wouldn't tell us what was scaring her. Each night, we would assure our daughter that she was safe and that she was just nervous in new surroundings. Then we would insist that she get to bed so she would be rested for school. Heather eventually stopped complaining about her bedroom. I did notice, however, that she never played in the basement. When I asked her why, she said she just didn't like it down there.

I must admit that, shortly after we moved into the house, I too began to feel uncomfortable in the basement. The basement stairs were at the back of the house, off the kitchen. The basement itself was partitioned into a laundry room, a general storage and work area, a tool/furnace room, and at the furthest end of the basement (under the front of the house) two more bedrooms. Since we didn't need the basement bedrooms, I turned one of them into a recreation area for the children.

Usually, everything was fine there and I could go down to do my laundry without any qualms. The washer and dryer were placed near the base of the steps and a peg-board wall divided this area from the furnace room. There were times, though, and it didn't matter if it was

8

day or night, that I would feel as if there were something malevolent close by. It was as if someone were standing in the furnace room, peering through the peg-board wall at me. This feeling could come at any time, and it didn't matter if I was alone in the house or not. I tried to tell myself that this was just my imagination, and I would continue to work on the laundry, although certainly at a faster pace. Now and again, the feeling would become too intense. It would overwhelm my determination and I would abandon what I was doing and run up the back stairs into the safety of the kitchen. If anyone was home, I didn't tell them what had happened, I simply pretended to be in a hurry to do something else.

Once upstairs, I would feel foolish. How could I tell my daughter not to be afraid if I was running away from something that couldn't possibly be there? Sometimes, I would gather up my courage and go back, turning on all the lights as I went, looking around, trying to prove to myself that there was no reason for my fear. But I didn't go down right away unless I knew that a family member was on the main floor, within shouting distance. As I would walk through the basement, the feeling of unease would return and increase as I made my way to the spare bedrooms at the far end. Once I had reached those rooms, I would begin my retreat to the basement stairs, turning out the lights of each room as I left it and then running to the safety of the next pool of light. Forget determination; forget courage and dignity; **let me out of here**!

At other times, I wouldn't even attempt to go back down for the rest of the day. On those occasions, the fear had been accompanied by the image of an ax flying through the air at my head as I ran up the stairs. The image of the ax, and the feeling of being pursued, always went away at the landing, but I never stopped running until I reached the kitchen. I learned later that I wasn't the only one who had imagined that specific weapon while fleeing.

I noticed that my husband seemed unaffected by the strange atmosphere in the basement. One day, Bill was down there trying to decide how to make the second bedroom into an area he could use for some electronics projects. The problem was that the boys periodically slept down there when we had house guests, so Bill suggested taking over the other room since the boys weren't using it as a rec. room, after all. We checked with them first and Howard said he was too busy with track after school to have friends over. Roger claimed he preferred to play outside and didn't have any use for the room. I was surprised since he'd enjoyed having friends over in our previous home, but I assumed his new set of friends preferred outdoor activities. So it was that the toys and games were removed from the basement, and Bill started to spend more time there himself.

My husband may have felt comfortable in the basement, but our dog certainly didn't. Knight usually followed Bill willingly everywhere around the house, except there. The dog would trail behind him down the stairs, but often wouldn't stay. He would run back and forth, from the kitchen to the basement room where Bill was working, unable to settle at Bill's feet.

To keep Knight company, we added another dog to our household; a wall-eyed Boston Terrier that we named Marty. This badly deformed dog would have been the perfect poster pet in a campaign against overbreeding animals. The two dogs shared a dislike for the basement and sometimes for other parts of the house. When they were in the basement, they would look at the unseeable and beat a hasty retreat; no time for barking then. Occasionally, they acted as though they had cornered an unseen quarry on the second floor landing, and would stand in different parts of the upstairs hall, staring at the same spot, barking and growling to try to scare it away. To the right of the landing, was a window seat where the dogs often sat; to the left, were the doors that led to the upstairs bedrooms. Was their quarry coming from the bedrooms, or trying to get to them?

Bill continued to build up his basement workroom. One day, he decided to mount some book shelves using adjustable brackets. In no time, he had a shelf in place and had placed his books on it. His intent was to add more shelves as he needed them. Once the job was complete, he put away his tools and came upstairs for coffee. Before he could pour a cup, we heard a crash. Bill went back to his work room and found the bookshelf on an angle, one end still leaning against its bracket and the other on the floor. The books were scattered. Assuming he'd been careless in centering the shelf, he replaced it, gathered the books off the floor and placed them back on the shelf. Returning for his coffee, he said, "I don't know why the books fell, but the shelf is secure now."

No sooner were the words spoken when there came another loud crash from the basement. Again, Bill investigated and saw that the shelf was on end, and the books were once more strewn across the room. To fall like that, the loaded shelf would have had to first slide several inches to the left, a feat that would have taken considerable strength if Bill had tried to do it himself.

After carefully replacing the shelf, making sure the edges came out a sufficient distance from each bracket, and adding the books carefully so that they were balanced properly on the shelf, he came upstairs once more. He told me what he'd done and added, "I shouldn't have to be that careful putting books on a shelf, but they'll stay this time."

Bill hadn't finished speaking when the now-familiar sound of shelf and books falling echoed up the stairs. "Nuts," he said, fed up with the whole thing, "I didn't need a shelf down there that badly." Nothing more was said on the subject, although Bill looked puzzled as he finally poured himself a cup of coffee. I noticed he didn't spend any more time in the basement that day.

Not long after Bill's abortive attempt to put up bookshelves, I started to have nastier experiences with the basement. I would be alone in the house, on the main floor, when a feeling of dread would overtake me. If it was daytime and the weather wasn't bad, I'd usually go out for a walk and find the feeling had passed when I returned. However, when going outside wasn't practical, I'd go into the living room and turn on the record player, hoping to drown out my fears with music. On more than one occasion, a hostile atmosphere developed in the house and I would find myself looking over at the far side of the kitchen, expecting to see something come up over the back stairs at any moment.

The negative atmosphere would continue to build, and if I still didn't leave, a male's menacing voice would seem to be speaking inside my head, saying, "Get out!" I'd hurry to the front hall and stand near the front door. Then a feeling of urgency would come at me, seeming to emanate from the stairs to the second floor. This was not an evil presence. It seemed to want me out of the house for my own safety. Depending on the weather, I might open the door and try to calm myself as I looked outside. Sometimes, in spite of the weather or other inconvenient circumstances, I would step out onto the porch, desperately hoping for someone to come home or for the atmosphere in the house to clear. These were the worst times for me in the house, worse even than being in the basement.

In spite of everything, I was determined to stay. This was my home and, except for these periods of negativity, I found it calm and inviting.

By the end of our first year in the house, I was taking college courses, the kids had made a lot of friends and weren't home much, and my husband's career kept him traveling a great deal of the time. We were all so busy over the next several years that we each became accustomed to, although not comfortable with, the weird behavior of the dogs and the odd sounds that we heard. We still didn't discuss the unnaturalness of it all with each other.

Then, one night in February of 1984, as Bill and I sat on the sofa reading, he asked me what I saw in the living room doorway. This doorway led to the front hall that was brightly lit at the time. I looked up, but saw nothing.

"Don't look straight at the doorway," Bill said. "Look across at the fireplace and observe the hall door with your peripheral vision." I did as he asked and tried again. Still nothing.

"Change places with me and try it," he suggested, still not telling what he thought I should see. I had been sitting on Bill's right, so changing places with him also put me closer to the door. I looked toward the fireplace, and could still see the hall door, but saw nothing unusual there. Then I picked up my book and sat as Bill had been sitting in that spot but, although I could see the hallway, I still couldn't see anything different.

"I can't see anything. What am I supposed to see?" I asked, totally mystified by my husband's preoccupation with the doorway.

"Let's change places again," he said. Once we were back in our original places, Bill picked up his book and, after a pause, said, "Yes. It's still there." Then he turned to me and explained what was going on. "I was sitting here reading my book when I got the feeling someone was waiting in the hallway. Out of the corner of my eye, I saw the figure of a man in shadow. He had on a fedora and a long overcoat and seemed to be leaning into the room slightly, waiting to be invited in. But when I looked straight at the hall door, he wasn't there. I went back to my reading, and he was back. Again, I looked directly at him and he was gone. This went on for about five minutes before I asked you to look too. I've been trying to figure out if it's a trick of the light, but I could still see it after we changed places and you haven't been able to see it at all."

"Who does it look like?" was all I could think to ask. Inside, I was glad I hadn't seen it, but I didn't doubt that Bill had.

"I can't think who he reminds me of," Bill replied as he turned back to have another look. "He's gone now. I can't even see him peripherally, but I know he was there."

"Have you seen him before?" I asked, relieved at last to know that someone else in the house was experiencing the inexplicable.

"No, I haven't," he said. "But there are a few odd sounds now and then, and sometimes I feel like I'm not alone in a room when I know that I am."

Bill, a biochemist by training, and a very rational person by nature, always looked for cause and effect, for logical answers to things that seem mysterious on the surface. But now, it seemed that there were things going on in the house that he couldn't explain. At last I had someone to talk to about all the strange things I'd experienced.

"I wonder if the kids have had any trouble here," I said.

"I wouldn't be surprised," said Bill, "especially Heather. She's never liked it here, and when we leave her at home alone in the evening, she turns on lights in every room. She even goes out of her way to turn the lights on in rooms she isn't using; the basement, for instance. I used to think she was just being thoughtless, but maybe she's afraid."

This seemed a good time to tell Bill about the cold October night when the basement spirit chased me out of the house. "Looking back on it," I said, "I don't think the spirit itself came upstairs, but it was so menacing that its mood took over the house. I can't remember being that afraid before or since." It had never been that extreme for Bill, but he didn't make fun of me for giving in to the terror.

We talked for a while longer and decided to say nothing to Heather and the boys for now. We'd just stay alert to their behavior and be ready to talk about the situation if any of them broached the subject. Not long after that, Heather did.

We had always assigned chores to the kids, rotating them so that no one was stuck with the same chore for too long. The boys particularly hated kitchen duty, however, and would often swap chores with Heather or pay her outright to do the dishes and clean up after supper. For a long time, she did a good job wiping the counters, putting away food, and getting all the dishes done. But shortly after Bill first saw the shadow, I noticed that Heather wasn't finishing the job. She'd leave condiments on the dining room table, leave pots and pans soaking in the sink instead of scrubbing them and putting them away, and she would sometimes neglect to wipe off the stove and the counters. The first few times this happened, I told her to go back and finish the job properly. When the problem continued, I thought perhaps she was too preoccupied with talking on the phone as she worked.

At 12, Heather was very involved with her friends. She had never been interested in reading books, as both of her brothers were. Her grades in school were not the best since she had to constantly struggle in order to read up on every subject. She did well, however, in any craft type project, as she had a real flair for color and design. Other than that, she did well in math, although the word problems took her a while to do. We tried to help her with her reading, even enrolling her in a special reading program after school, but she had a mental block on this topic. It would be a few years before her reading would improve, once she realized it held her back when she was looking for part-time work. Instead, she preferred going to dancing lessons after school or working on crafts. But even more than these pursuits, Heather preferred shopping with her friends, or talking to them by the hour. When they weren't out together, the phone line was like an umbilical cord connecting her to them.

In order to encourage her to spend more time on her school work in the evenings, we restricted our daughter's social life to evening phone calls after school on weekdays. Now, as I entered the kitchen with her and looked at the half-completed cleanup, I was exasperated. It seemed that her telephonic social life was interfering with her household chores, so I told Heather it was time we suspended her phone privileges. With that dire threat hanging over our daughter's head, she finally told me what was bothering her.

"It seems like every time supper's over, everyone takes off. The boys go to their room or out with friends, Dad goes into the library to work on the computer, and you go out or upstairs to study. I'm left alone in the kitchen and it makes me nervous" Heather was pacing in the kitchen as she said this, and her voice was rising with each word she spoke.

"Lower your voice, Heather, I can hear you just fine," I said, not too pleased with her either at the moment.

Heather stopped pacing and lowered her voice, but there was still defiance in it as she stood in front of me and continued. "I always hated the basement, so having the basement stairs at the back of the kitchen bothers me. And...well, you're not going to believe this, but lately, I've been getting the feeling that someone's in the living room. At first, I only saw it out of the corner of my eye when I went into the dining room to clear the table. It looked like a man was standing in the living room, near the front hall door, watching me. I just about jumped out of my skin every time I saw him. But when I looked straight into the living room, he'd be gone."

Heather paused, waiting for me to tell her she was just imagining things, but I didn't. "When did this start?" I asked, surprised she hadn't told me the first time she saw it. I sat down at the kitchen table to ease the tension between us.

"It's been almost a year now, I guess," she replied, sitting down across from me, her voice no longer defiant. "But lately, while I'm going back and forth through the kitchen, I sometimes see him. He's been moving further into the living room these last few weeks. I know you'll think I'm nuts, but I really see him and he's getting closer to the dining room all the time. I feel trapped in the kitchen between the basement stairs and him."

I told my daughter that I didn't think she was crazy, that her father had seen it, too. Then I asked what the man looked like.

"He's kind of tall and slim," she said after some thought, "It seemed like he was wearing a long coat; it hung loose, no belt. He also had on a hat."

"What kind of hat was he wearing?" I asked.

"The kind of hat Grandpa had on in an old picture you once showed me. You know, a Dick Tracy kind of hat." So, Heather had given me the same description of the man that Bill had.

"Have you ever told your brothers about the man or about your fear of the basement," I asked.

"What? And have them tease me about it forever?" she asked, looking at me as though I'd lost my senses. "No way!" Heather stood up and went over to the sink where a pile of soaking pans was waiting. "I hate this house," she said, as I got up from the table. "I wish we would just move away."

Pausing at the kitchen doorway, I said, "It's not that easy just to sell up and move on every time there's a problem. Besides, what if the weirdness follows us to the next house?" Heather muttered something under her breath as I left the room.

"It's time I talked to Roger and Howard," I thought. "At this rate, I'll be surprised if they haven't had any unusual experiences here." Curiosity was beginning to replace my fear of the unknown source of all this activity. We seemed to have quite a few spirits in the house. The one upstairs made me feel protected, but why didn't Heather feel safe there? What did the dogs bark at on the upstairs landing? Was it the spirit of the old woman that I felt in our room, or was there another one? Now there seemed to be a Dick Tracy type on the main floor. But what was in the basement? Were these spirits able to move freely about the house, or were they confined to specific areas somehow? I wondered what we'd have to do to get rid of the frightening spirits.

18

A few days after my talk with Heather, I had an opportunity to speak with Howard when he came home from his part-time job. Everyone else was asleep, so I went down to talk to him while he fixed himself a late night snack. After we had chatted for a while about the day's events, I decided to ask about his experiences with the house. "I've been wondering if you've ever had anything odd happen to you since we moved into this house," I said, jumping into the conversation with both feet.

Howard, who was 17 years old by this time, did well in school, was involved in extracurricular activities, and held down a part-time job. Although he dated a lot, he still found time for his friends. No matter what time he came in from work or partying, however, he was an early riser who seldom missed school. He was also an avid reader of science fiction who loved to play Dungeons and Dragons with his brother and their friends. He would get caught up in the fantasy of a story or a game, and thoroughly enjoy himself, but he was able to separate these pursuits from reality.

Howard thought about my question for a moment and then asked, "What do you mean by odd?"

"Well, is there anything you've heard or seen that you can't explain; or maybe some odd feeling that you've had when you're alone in some part of the house?" I said, being careful not to be too specific.

"Have you?" Howard asked. He put down his partially eaten sandwich and opened the fridge where he proceeded to look around for another can of pop. I had the feeling he was looking for the pop as a way to keep from looking at me until I could answer his question.

"Well," I said, "I've heard some noises I couldn't account for, over the years. And lately, I found out that your father and sister have been seeing something strange. You know your sister never liked this house

19

and now she tells me that it's because it feels weird to her."

Howard sat down with his pop and thought for a moment before speaking. "So Dad's had some odd things happen to him, too." He seemed to relax a little more at the thought that his father was accepting his own experiences as a mystery. "There have been times in our bedroom when the room will get cold for no reason and the small closet door will come open on its own," Howard said, at last. "It doesn't happen all the time, but when I know someone is coming over, I put something in front of that door to keep it closed. At first I didn't think of that, but several of my friends looked real scared when they saw the door open by itself, so I don't take chances anymore."

"Did you say anything to your friends about it when it happened," I asked, curious to see if he had talked to anyone else about the strange goings on.

"Nah. They'd just look and say 'Weird,' or something, but they never stayed in the room long after the door opened. In fact," said Howard, "some of them never came back into our house."

"Anything else?" I asked.

"Well," Howard continued reluctantly. "I used to feel like there was something strange about the library, so I close that door at night. I never actually had anything happen there; it was just a feeling." The boys slept in a bedroom on the main floor, near the dining room. There was a short hallway off the dining room, which led to a bathroom, a library, and their bedroom.

"What about the basement?" I asked. "You never seemed to spend much time down there."

"To tell you the truth, Mom, the whole house feels uncomfortable some days, but other times, things are fine. I don't know what happens to make the difference. Sometimes, when I've been down there by myself, I'd get the feeling that I'd better get out in a hurry. I'd be running by the time I reached the stairs. I've even thought that an ax was flying through the air after me."

This last remark startled me. I'd had the same experience, but hadn't told anyone. I'd always thought it was my imagination working overtime. Now, I wasn't so sure. But why an ax? There's no ax in the basement, so why should we both have imagined one? Before I could make any comments, Howard continued, "And then there's the times I've slept in the basement bedroom because we've had company. Sometimes, when I sleep in the top bunk, I wake up feeling like I'd better not open my eyes, or move my arms out of the bed even to buzz the intercom. I just keep my eyes shut and tell myself it's okay. Eventually, the feeling goes away." Howard seemed embarrassed to be talking about this, and stood up from the table. "If that's all, Mom, I think I'd better get some sleep now."

"Just one more thing," I said, my curiosity making me ignore his wish to end the discussion. "What happens when you sleep on the bottom bunk?"

"Oh, I wouldn't sleep there," he replied. "The top bunk's the only place that feels safe down there." With that, he kissed me goodnight and we both headed for our rooms.

"What on earth is going on here?" I thought as I climbed the stairs. "And why have we all waited so long to talk about it?" I'd always enjoyed working on puzzles, but finding a solution to what was taking place in our house was going to be very challenging. I wondered what Roger would have to say when I had a chance to talk to him.

The following Saturday, I had my opportunity. At fifteen, my younger son Roger was very much a night owl; he always had been. He worked part-time at a fast

21

food place and was forever asking for the late shift so he could sleep in. When he wasn't working, he would hang out with friends until his curfew, and then stay awake half the night reading. He'd read books on a wide variety of topics, from science fiction to ancient history; he was interested in everything, except school. It fell to me to make sure he was up in time for school during the week, but on the weekend, I would let him sleep longer. It really didn't matter what time I got my son out of bed, since his mind didn't engage the real world much before noon.

At 11 a.m. on this particular morning, I went into his room for the third time and said, "Roger, I want you up and into the shower now. I have a lot to do today and I want to talk to you before I go out." Saying this, I hauled the covers off him and opened his blinds.

"Just five more minutes, Mom," he mumbled, trying to bury his head in his pillow to block out the light.

"Now," I said, hauling on his arm, as if I could actually make him get up. Roger was tall and lanky, and shouldn't have been too hard to move, but he was also a dead weight at that moment. I yanked on his arm, more to pull him out of his dreams than out of his bed.

"All right! All right," he said. Standing at last, he staggered off in the direction of the bathroom. "You'd think a person could get a little sleep around here," he muttered. I went off to the kitchen to prepare a pot of coffee. A half hour later, Roger came into the dining room, clean and dressed, and somewhat alert.

"What's up?" he asked, as he prepared a large bowl of cereal. I handed him a cup of coffee, and told him some of the things the rest of us had experienced in the house. By the time I'd finished bringing him up to date, Roger was eating a last slice of toast and starting on his second cup of coffee. Unlike his brother, Howard, who didn't like to talk about it, Roger needed no prompting to tell what he'd experienced.

"It's funny," he said, "we never did talk about it, but we all knew. Without discussing it, Howard and I both used to put things in front of our bedroom closet door to keep it from opening when we had friends over. We'd gotten used to it ourselves, but there was no sense scaring anyone else. There were times when we would check over the door to see if there was a reason it wouldn't stay closed. There wasn't. We never talked about what really might be happening, but once I thought I saw the door knob turning on its own before the door opened."

"And then there was the basement," Roger continued. "When I was a kid, I tried to use the playroom you made for us down there, but it felt really weird. After a few times alone, I decided I'd only go down there when I had friends over. We'd be playing when a sinister feeling would come, sometimes the room would get really cold, and we'd all decide to leave the basement at once." Roger paused for a moment and then added, "A lot of times, when I was running for the stairs, I had the impression that something sharp was flying through the air and might hit me in the back."

That image again! Roger, hadn't mentioned an ax, but, without the least sign of hesitation or embarrassment, he'd recounted a similar experience. "I've had thoughts like that too," I said, nodding slowly. "What do you mean by something sharp, though?"

"I don't really know," Roger replied, after thinking about it for a few moments. "It could have been a knife, I suppose, although I was never really sure; I only knew I might get stuck in the back with something."

Now that I knew how frightened he'd been of the basement, I had to ask, "But you've slept in the bunks down there when we've had company. With all the scares you've had down there, how could you stand it?"

"Well...," he said, and then paused, staring off into the distance for a moment before continuing. "It helped a bit if Howard was sleeping there, too. But there were times when I'd wake up in the night with the feeling that I'd better not open my eyes, that something evil was in the room. If I was on the bottom bunk, I also had the impression that a hand was reaching down from the upper bunk to grab me. I'd stay very still and just pray for it to go away. Eventually, it would pass, but I didn't get much sleep after that. If I was on the top bunk, I just knew that I'd better not open my eyes or try to get out of bed." Roger thought for a moment and then added, "Of course, if Howard was with me, he always insisted on taking the top bunk. Guess he didn't like the bottom one, either."

"What about the rest of the house?" I asked. "Do you have any problems there?"

"In case you haven't noticed, Mom," he replied, "I seldom ever go to the second floor. I don't feel welcome up there. It isn't scary, like the basement can be; I just don't like it. I used to like sitting in the window seat; it was quiet there. But sometimes, for no reason, it would start to feel really cold, and I'd feel like I wasn't alone." Roger thought for a moment, and then went on, "As for the main floor, other than our bedroom, I've had a few times where I started to go into the library to get a book, and I saw a man sitting in Dad's chair, out of the corner of my eye."

"What'd he look like?" I asked. Just then, the phone rang and Roger spent the next few minutes making plans with a friend of his. When he finally hung up, I asked again what the man looked like.

"I didn't see much," he replied. "He was sitting down, so what I really noticed was that he had a hat on.

24

The kind that men used to wear in the old gangster movies on TV."

"A fedora?" I asked.

"Yeah, that's it," said Roger, grabbing his jacket. "Well, I gotta go now. Let's talk about this some more later."

"It wouldn't bother you to talk about it again?" I asked, remembering how reluctant Howard had been to discuss it and how upset it made Heather.

"Heck no!" said Roger, with a grin, "It's about time we all said what we've been thinking. And anyway, I think it's pretty interesting." With that, my younger son was out the door and I was left to wonder why my three kids would have such different reactions. They'd all had pretty similar experiences; odd that no two of them felt alike.

The boys seemed to have a spirit in their bedroom that opened their closet door. Was it the Dick Tracy spirit, or another one? Why wasn't Roger welcome upstairs? He'd mentioned feeling cold by the window seat, and yet the dogs spent a lot of time there. Did the dogs ever feel cold there? Is that what upset them and made them bark on the landing sometimes? I began to wonder if the old woman from our room sometimes wandered into the hall and created a coldness that upset the dogs and made them bark.

"Will it be any easier to deal with now that we've all talked about it?" I wondered. Over time I was to find that discussing the unusual occurrences in our house was a mixed blessing. On the one hand, we knew we weren't crazy when these feelings came over us; on the other hand, we could no longer ignore the phenomena by attributing them to our own overactive imaginations.

25

Chapter 2

Once we had all acknowledged that something odd was taking place in the house, we began to recognize a pattern to the disturbances. There would be stretches of time during which the house was quiet; by that, I mean no one saw, heard, or felt anything out of the ordinary. Then, over a period of days or weeks, a tension would build up in the atmosphere. Doors would open and close and footsteps could be heard on the second floor, when no one was up there. The dogs would begin barking at unseen intruders on the front stairs, and they would refuse to stay in the basement if they followed anyone down there. The old feeling of being watched, and being unwelcome, would return to any of us who ventured down to do laundry, or fetch food from the freezer located near the furnace room. Eventually, we would have to discuss what was happening, and the activity would slowly subside.

During one of these eerie periods, Bill was reading on the sofa when he noticed the Dick Tracy-like shadow in the dining room. He watched it out of the corner of his eye for a few moments. Just then, Heather entered the room and stood on the same spot occupied by the shadow. Bill turned to speak to her, intending to ask if she was feeling anything odd.

"Heather," he said, calmly, "Do you...," But before he could finish asking his question, she let out a yelp and jumped backwards.

"What's the matter?" Bill asked her.

"I don't know," she said. "I just came in and all of a sudden the spot where I was standing felt really cold. It sent shivers all through my body."

Because they were looking directly at the spot where the shadow had appeared, neither Bill nor Heather could see him. "Dick Tracy was standing there before you came in," he explained "You stepped directly onto the same spot. I just wondered what you felt."

"I hate this!" she said, hurrying into the living room to sit close to Bill. He turned his head slightly to see if he could catch a glimpse of the shadow again, but he couldn't.

"Don't worry, it's gone now," he said. But she would not be so easily reassured and spent the next hour listening to her favorite music played loudly on the radio. This made reading difficult for Bill, but he knew she needed the comfort of his company, so he turned the volume down a little and did his best to finish what he was reading.

That night was the last time Bill ever saw the Dick Tracy shadow. Roger and Heather, on the other hand, began to see it more clearly, and eventually were able to look directly at it.

Around the time that Bill first saw Dick Tracy, I also noticed that the spirit in our bedroom was becoming stronger. She made her presence felt in more physical ways, rather than just the noises that we had first experienced. One night, as I lay in bed, worried about a problem involving one of our children, I felt a hand gently come to rest on my arm, as if to reassure me that all would be well. This sensation lasted for less than a minute, and left me feeling comforted, rather than frightened.

By comparing experiences like this, we began to realize that the house was most likely to be in an uproar when something serious was happening to someone in our family. The spirit in our bedroom, for instance, used to raise a ruckus whenever we needed to check into what our children were up to.

In November of 1984, Howard entered the Navy and, by spring of 1985, was stationed in Newport News, Virginia. On one occasion that spring, Heather and Roger were both staying overnight at friends' homes, and Bill and I were home alone. Our dog, Marty, had developed the annoying habit of snoring loudly near the foot of our bed, so, since we were very tired, my husband decided to put her in the hall. Because our bedroom door latch was broken, Bill had to lock the door to keep it closed. I awoke when I heard the bedroom door creak open. The illuminated numbers on our alarm clock showed that it was 2:03 a.m. The house was in darkness, and the dogs weren't barking, so I knew that neither one of our kids had returned home unexpectedly. Feeling uneasy, I roused my husband and asked him if he had unlocked the door.

Bill thought about it and said, "Maybe I didn't turn the lock all the way, and it just came open." He got up and relocked the door, saying, "That should stay shut now." We were both tired and fell immediately back to sleep. Not long after, however, I woke up to find that the door was open and Marty was in our room snoring away. Again, I woke Bill who insisted he had definitely set the lock properly and had not been up since. Muttering under his breath, he put the dog back in the hall, and locked the door. He even rattled the door knob to make sure the door was truly locked. Finally satisfied that the door would not open again, Bill returned to bed. In no time, he was fast asleep; but I was determined to find out what was going on and so I forced myself to stay awake. After a few minutes, there were three loud thumps on the door. Marty was small and in such poor physical shape that she could not have been the cause of this violent pounding. I was terrified by what was happening, but, inexplicably, I immediately fell asleep. When we woke in the morning, the door was once again wide open.

That day, I checked with each of my children to see if they had anything troubling that they needed to talk to us about. Roger then told us that he and his friend had gone into Chicago the night before, after his friend's parents went to bed. They had become lost in a rough part of the city. Each street they turned down, in an effort to find their way out, led them into more forbidding territory. By the time they got back to the highway, they were both very frightened and my son was wishing fervently that he was home in his own bed. When they'd first realized they were lost, it was two o'clock in the morning.

As the years went by, the unusual activity continued. Although some of our experiences still frightened us, most seemed harmless. We grew accustomed to the spirits, and casually referred to them as "the other family." But one interesting new phenomenon did develop. There was a patch on the front lawn, under our white pine tree, where grass stopped growing. We did everything we could to fix it. We even replaced the lawn and had a company tend our lawn for a year. During that time the grass grew, but eventually, the bald patch was back, this time in the size and shape of a child's small casket. We were all disturbed by this, but we hid our concern with jokes. At one point, Roger even went into the front yard with a long rod to see if he could locate anything a few feet below the surface. He couldn't. He offered to dig up that patch to find out if a grave was actually there. I wouldn't let him do that. We hadn't let the neighbors know about our spirits, and I wasn't about to provoke their curiosity. So we decided it was best to chalk the shape up to coincidence, much like seeing familiar shapes in clouds and knowing they didn't really mean anything.

Whenever Howard came home on leave, he did his best to avoid talking about the house, preferring to deny that anything had ever really happened. Heather remained as unhappy as ever that we wouldn't move, and spent as little time as possible at home. Roger read up on the supernatural to try to understand what was happening. But he wanted to make sure that he didn't automatically blame everything that happened on spirits, so he always looked for logical explanations for our experiences, without too much success. Bill and I would joke that, while our teenagers could open the fridge door and inhale all the food within seconds, at least the other family didn't add to our grocery or utility bills. That wasn't exactly true; they did add to our electric bill because Heather continued to turn on every light in the house when she was home alone.

In the fall of 1988, Roger entered the Army one month before Howard was to leave the Navy. During that month, my life-long friend, Sue, came to visit with her daughter, Charlotte. Sue was a businesswoman who was not given to nervous episodes. She slept in the bedroom on the main floor while Charlotte shared Heather's upstairs room. After they had been with us for a few days, I came down one morning to find Sue sitting in the dining room with a cup of coffee.

"I had the most horrible experience in that room last night," she told me. "It started with a bad dream about my mother." Sue's mother, a very religious woman, had died several years earlier. "In the dream, my mother came to see me. At first, I was glad to see her; but then I noticed how mean she was to other people in the dream; how she enjoyed humiliating them and hurting them. She had turned into an evil person. Even though I was dreaming, I was terrified. I told her that she was dead and had to go back where she came from. But she said she wanted to stay with me, and wouldn't go. As I kept insisting that she had to leave, I had the feeling that she was growing even more evil. Finally, in spite of her screaming that she wanted to stay, she melted down into a kind of lump that spread across the floor as a sticky goop. The last thing to disappear was her face. To the end she was screaming, insisting that she wouldn't leave." Sue stopped talking for a moment while she lit a cigarette and took a sip of her coffee.

"What do you suppose that dream meant?" I asked, assuming that it would represent some problem that Sue may have had recently.

"Wait," Sue said, "There's more. In the dream, I tried to get rid of this blob, without actually touching it, because I felt it would harm me if I came into contact with it. I started vacuuming it when, suddenly, there was a young boy in the room who offered to help. But he touched the goop, and before I could wipe it off of him, he began to grow. In seconds he was over seven feet tall, with odd lumps all over his body. He oozed evil from every pore. Before I could run away, he grabbed my arm, lifted me off my feet like I was a rag doll, and pulled me through a doorway. I knew I was doomed."

Sue sat still for a moment thinking over her dream. She shivered a little and then went on. "I woke up before anything else could happen. My eyes were still closed, but I could feel evil in the room with me. My heart was pounding in my chest; I could even feel the pulse in my neck throbbing. I knew I'd better not open my eyes, so I lay there reciting the 23rd psalm. By the time the feeling went away and I felt I could safely look around the room, it was light out. I knew I'd never get back to sleep, so I got up and fixed myself a cup of coffee. I've been up ever since."

"I'm sorry, Sue," I said, upset that the negativity in the house was also affecting our guests. "The boys have had similar feelings of evil in the basement bedroom, but it never occurred to me that you would feel anything like that on this floor. I should have warned you." Then I told Sue about our adventures in the house. She had visited before without incident, so this was new to her.

"You should get out of here," she said when I'd finished. "Something's really wrong." Ever since, Sue has said, on a regular basis, "I don't know how you can stay there. I wish you'd move." But I was determined to find a solution to this problem. I began to read more about haunted houses, hoping to find an answer, but those accounts always seemed to end with people leaving their homes. This was not an acceptable solution to me.

Once Howard's term in the Navy was completed, he came home, got a job and eventually moved out on his own. In 1990, he married a girl he'd met in Virginia, and then moved there with her before their first son was born.

After Howard and his family had moved away, we acquired a third dog; a mixed breed that had been abandoned along with a litter of seven other puppies. For a time, the house was quiet: just Heather, Bill and I, and the dogs in it. Shay, our new pup, got along well with us and the older two dogs, but he was very shy around most other people and animals. Since the pup wanted to chew everything in sight, including the living room furniture, Bill decided to build a room-sized cage for him in the basement, not far from the stairs. Shay could stay in that cage during the day when no one was home. Our daughter was concerned about us confining Shay to the basement. She told me that she'd heard a child's laughter coming from the corner where Bill was building and was concerned that the spirits would drive the poor puppy crazy.

I didn't like the idea of leaving a dog there either, but I couldn't think of anywhere else he could be kept. He was still teething and had already inflicted a great deal of damage on the wooden legs and pedestals of our furniture. If we confined him to a room on the main floor, he scratched unceasingly on the doors, making deep gouges in the oak. We'd tried placing a baby gate in the kitchen doorway to keep him away from the furniture, but soon he was able to jump over the gate from a sitting position. The room Bill was building in the basement seemed to be the only answer.

When the cage was complete, we began leaving him in there during the day. The dog didn't stay put. Several times, when Bill came home at lunch time, he found Shay on the loose in the main part of the house. When he took him back into the basement, the door to the cage would be unlocked and wide open. On one occasion, he put Shay in the cage after lunch and the dog came up the stairs before Bill could even leave the house. When Bill investigated, he discovered that the cage door was still shut and locked! It was a floor to ceiling structure; the door was the only way out.

In desperation, he put the dog back in the cage and announced to the room, "If I can't keep Shay in the cage, we can't keep him." The dog never did get loose after that. After a few months, he'd learned not to chew up the furniture, and he no longer had to be locked up during the day.

Shay soon grew to be huge, weighing over 100 pounds, and commanded respect by virtue of his size. But, like Marty and Knight, he had a fear of the basement, and sometimes refused to go down there, even in our company.

By the time Roger left the Army in 1991, Heather had a family of her own. She and her baby daughter, Alex, were living with us, in the boys' old bedroom on the main floor. The room was very cramped with a double bed, a dresser, and a crib, plus assorted baby paraphernalia. I asked Heather why she didn't want to use her old room on the second floor, since it was much larger. It also made sense that, since she was afraid in the house anyway, she might feel safer sleeping upstairs with us.

"I never want to sleep in that room again!" she said, emphatically. "The first night we were here, I saw a soldier in the closet. He was dressed in a very old style uniform; from the Civil War, I think. I knew you wouldn't believe me, so I never told you about him. But that was why I was so afraid up there as a kid. Every now and again he still shows up," she continued, "and I don't want him scaring Alex."

"Oh great!" I thought. "That means there are at least two ghosts upstairs; three, if the one in the window seat isn't the old woman."

"What makes you think you'll be any better off down here?" I asked.

"At least down here, I can leave all the lights on if I want and not disturb anybody's sleep," she replied. "If I get too nervous, I can always go into the living room and watch TV." Poor Heather; she was to have many unsettling experiences in that bedroom before she moved out of the house for the last time.

Meanwhile, Roger came home from the Army expecting to move back into his bedroom. "Sorry Son," I said, "I know you don't like the second floor, but Heather and Alex have already claimed your old room." He grudgingly moved into the upstairs bedroom after trying unsuccessfully to talk Heather into returning to it herself.

Within a week of moving home, Roger sat down with me one evening and said, "You know Mom, I never liked the second floor. I never felt welcome there. But, since I've come back, I feel just fine upstairs. Maybe it's because I've been a soldier, so I fit in. Because, Mom, there's a Civil War soldier in the closet. I saw him last night." Roger sat there, grinning, expecting me to be surprised, I guess.

"I know about the soldier," I told him. "Heather used to see him there. That's why she wanted to move into your old room." Now it was Roger's turn to be surprised.

Heather and her daughter, Alex, lived with us periodically from 1991 to 1993. Each time they moved in, Heather refused to occupy her old room upstairs. But, even though she felt more comfortable in the main floor bedroom, she was unnerved by her baby's behavior. "Alex looks out between the bars of her crib and her eyes move around as if she's watching something that I can't see; then she'll goo and laugh at whatever it is. And, as if that weren't enough, sometimes her musical toys will start playing on their own."

I understood what Heather was talking about. On more than one occasion, my husband and I would be sitting, reading in the living room and Alex's tiny, musical horse would begin to play in her playpen, even when she wasn't there. This particular toy had a button on the front that had to be pressed to start the music. Three nursery songs would play in a row, and then the music would stop until the button was pressed again. We noticed that, when the music started up on its own, the three songs would play at least three times in a row before stopping.

On several occasions, when Alex's father, Jason, came by to visit the baby, he'd be in the hall, heading for the dining room and would catch sight of a little boy with blond hair running quickly through the dining room, past the hall door. Because the little boy would run very quickly, Jason dubbed him "the track star."

I saw this child myself, but only once. I was standing in the dining room when I happened to look toward the large window on the other side of the room. This window covers most of one dining room wall, with just a few inches of wall near the ceiling and two feet between the window and the floor. Glancing out, I saw the head, arms, and torso of a little blond-haired boy running past the window on his way from the backyard to the street. I looked away, and then realized that even an adult walking past the window would only have been visible as far as the shoulders or upper chest. How could I have seen so much of the child?

I hurried to the living room window, where I could see the front yard, and looked around, but no little boy was in sight. I'd assumed that he was outside because his legs were missing from my view. But what if the light from the window had obscured my vision, so that I couldn't see his legs against the darker wall?

After comparing notes with Jason, I realized I had probably seen "the track star." If so, was this the spirit who played with Alex and her toys? Could it also be the spirit that Heather had once heard laughing in the basement while Bill was building the cage for Shay. If it was the same spirit, it was the first one I knew of that wasn't confined to just one floor in this house.

When Alex was about six months old, Jason came to visit, and he and Heather began to discuss a possible reconciliation. As they sat on her bed, talking, the brass floor lamp in her room turned on. Heather was startled by this and jumped. "How'd that happen?" she wondered aloud.

"Oh, don't worry about it," Jason said, reaching over to turn the lamp off. "The switch is hard to turn. Maybe it wasn't turned all the way and gradually slipped back into the on position." Satisfied with this explanation, they resumed their conversation. After a few minutes, the light turned on again.

"There it goes again," said Heather, growing more nervous. She reached over and turned the switch off once more.

"Look, it must just have a faulty switch. If it'll make you happy, I'll pull the plug and then the light can't turn on again," Jason said. But when he went around the side of the bed to unplug it, he discovered that the lamp was already unplugged. "Get the baby, Heather," he said, now as spooked as she was. "We're going for a ride." Heather dressed the baby quickly and they left the house. They went for a long drive while Heather tried to calm down so they could return.

A few nights later, Jason called Heather and they talked until late into the night. Just after Heather hung up, she got the now familiar feeling that something evil was in the room. As she later explained it to me, "I was usually asleep when this evil feeling would come. I'd wake up knowing that I shouldn't open my eyes. Eventually, the feeling would go away. But this time, I was wide awake, and I looked around the room. There was a man crouched in the corner by the closet. As I looked at him, he slowly stood up. He was very tall and all dressed in black. I couldn't see his face, though, because he had something like a hood up around his head and his hand held the cloth together in front of his face. I thought he was a monk or something. I just stared at him, terrified. I wanted to scream, or run, but I couldn't move. Finally, he just faded away." I was upset for my daughter as she related this story. It was clear that she'd been terrified. I would have been too in her place. It seemed that every floor in this house held something terrifying for her. Not long after she told me about the crouched man, Heather and Jason reconciled, and she and the baby moved out.

With his sister gone, Roger quickly reclaimed the main floor bedroom. He never did see the spirit she'd seen in that room. In fact, the house was quiet for a few months. Then one night, while Bill was away on business, I was in bed, reading when I heard my son come in. It was 11:30 but, since we hadn't had a chance to talk in a while, I went downstairs to keep him company while he had his usual snack/meal. By the time he'd finished eating, we were well into a discussion of politics or something equally weighty, so we adjourned to the living room to continue in comfort. Shay was asleep upstairs, while Marty and Knight slept peacefully at our feet. One topic led to another, and before we knew it, several hours had passed. Suddenly, from the basement, we heard a dog howl, as if in extreme distress. The noise seemed to go on forever, growing louder and more pitiful. Roger and I just looked at each other, our eyes wide; I could feel the hair on the back of my neck rising. Then the sound stopped. It was dead quiet in the room. Our dogs, who would normally wake up and yap at the least little sound, remained fast asleep.

"Where do you think that came from?" asked Roger, standing up at last.

"I'd swear it came from the basement, just under the kitchen stairs," I said. Roger went into the kitchen and looked out the window at the darkened back yards around us. There was no sign of a dog anywhere. All was silent.

"I could have sworn it came from the basement, too," he said. "But how? All our dogs are up here."

I had to agree, but I noticed neither one of us was suggesting that we go into the basement to investigate. Among other things, that would mean opening the door to the dreaded "N.U.S." room. This was a room, slightly larger than a closet, that housed our sump pump. It must have been a private meeting place for children who had once lived in our house. On the door, the letters N.U.S. had been drawn. Inside the room, the floor was all broken up. To the left of the door, someone had nailed up an old quilt, while letters and words, painted in blue by a childish hand, were scrawled all over the remaining walls. To the right of the door, at the far end of the room, there was a small, dark, cobweb-laden crawl space that led under the kitchen stairs. None of our children ever ventured into it.

"At least it stopped," I said. "I don't know which of us was more scared when the howling started. I know I felt at least as alarmed as you looked."

"Yeah," said Roger, "that was scary all right." He stopped trying to find the cause of the noise outside the house. "Well, I think we'd better just go to bed," he said. I agreed and with that, he turned off the downstairs lights, while I took the dogs upstairs.

We never did hear the dog howl again, much to my relief, but we remained aware of it. Off and on over the next few years, several of us, including my two daughters-in-law, would hear a phantom dog roaming

40

through the basement or the main floor of the house. But, for some reason, like the little boy's spirit, it never went upstairs to our bedroom. There were times when we'd feel a pesky dog sniffing at our feet as we worked at the kitchen table, only to find there was no dog there when we looked down. One evening, when Roger was first dating his wife, Jennifer, he brought her to the house to watch videos. They were alone in the house when they heard a dog pacing the hallway off the dining room. Growing more agitated by his confinement, the dog began sniffing under the doorway, trying to find a way out. Thinking Shay had accidentally been shut in, Jennifer opened the door to let him out. It was quiet in the hall. There was no dog there. This was her first experience with the house and, although it made her feel nervous, she tried to take it in stride because she saw that it intrigued, rather than frightened, Roger. "I wouldn't stay on my own in your house, though," she has since told me.

Eventually, Roger moved into his own apartment and I converted the main floor bedroom into an office. In June of 1992, Howard returned alone from Virginia to take a new job. He intended to save money towards a nice apartment for his family by moving in with us. His wife, Kathy, and son Nick came for a 10-day visit that August. To give them more privacy, I let them use my office as their bedroom. During this visit, Kathy had her first experience with the "other family."

It was after midnight. The lights were all out, and Howard and Kathy were drifting off to sleep when she heard a dog scratching at the hall door, near the bedroom. Kathy nervously prodded Howard and whispered, "Howard, what's that in the hall?"

Howard had his back to the door, so he raised himself up on his elbow and listened for a moment. "Oh, it's just Shay," he said sleepily and lay back down. In no time, he was snoring. Kathy did her best to get to sleep herself, but, although she couldn't see it, she had the unnerving feeling that there was a large dog silently watching them from the darkness of the hall. Then she remembered that we had taken all the dogs upstairs with us and closed the upstairs doors.

"This can't be Shay!" she thought and lay there, paralyzed with fear, unwilling even to try to rouse Howard again. Kathy recalled the strange incidents of the last few days when she'd been alone in the kitchen preparing a meal. On one occasion, she'd felt and heard a dog at her feet; later, she'd heard a dog scratching on the other side of the closed kitchen door. Each time, when she looked for the dog who'd been making the noise, she found nothing. It startled her at the time, but she decided she must have been mistaken about the nature of the sounds she'd heard. But this time, both she and Howard had heard the dog in the hall! Kathy was unable to sleep for the rest of the night. In the morning when she told him about it, Howard filled her in on some of the odd things that'd happened here over the years.

"If he'd told me before, I would've insisted that we stay in a hotel," she told me later. "I never used to believe in spirits. I'd think you were all crazy if I hadn't seen it for myself." As it was, she left the house each day with their son, Nick, and stayed out shopping and sight-seeing until it was time for us all to come home from work. Indeed, that visit was the last time Kathy slept in our house.

After Kathy and Nick returned to Virginia, Howard moved back upstairs into Heather's old bedroom. For a few months, the house was quiet, and then the feeling of an unseen presence close by, and noises we couldn't account for, built up the tension in the atmosphere once more. One night in October, while Bill was away, I went to bed a little early. I was still awake, reading, when Howard came home at 10:30. He saw that my light was on and stopped in to talk to me. While we were chatting, Shay began to pace between us and the hall door. It was clear that he needed to be put outside and Howard volunteered to do it, since he was going downstairs to fix himself a snack anyway.

"It's been raining today, so the yard will be muddy," I said. "Shay's feet will be all covered in muck when he gets in, so be sure to send him into the basement to run around until his feet are dry. He knows he has to do this when his feet are wet, so he shouldn't give you any trouble." Howard took Shay downstairs and, within a few minutes, I began to feel very uneasy. Without knowing why, I knew something was wrong and I decided I'd better check on Howard. Before I had time to act on my thoughts, Howard reappeared looking very pale. He crossed his arms and stood in the doorway with his legs locked, as though bracing himself.

"The weirdest thing just happened downstairs," he said. "I let Shay out and when he came in his feet were very muddy, so I turned the light on in the basement and pointed for him to go down. At first Shay tried to slink up the stairs to the kitchen, but I shouted at him and he finally went downstairs. He no sooner hit the bottom step when he shot right back up, passed me on the landing, and cowered at the top of the stairs. I guess he knew better than to go into the kitchen with muddy feet, but he certainly didn't want to go into the basement."

"Sometimes, he gets spooked, and you have to go down with him," I said. As I spoke, Shay slunk into the bedroom and went into a corner where he curled up as small as he could.

"Oh, I tried that, too," Howard said. "I went down the stairs, dragging him behind me by the collar. Man, is he hard to move when he's scared!" he added, glaring over at the dog.

"Well at least you got him down there," I said.

"Not for long," Howard continued, looking, in disgust, at our 100 pound dog. "We made it to the bottom of the steps, and I let go of him so he could run around, but he turned and raced back up to the landing. I yelled at him to come back, but he just stayed there, cowering; his eyes were rolling in his head, he was so scared. Then, I felt two hands on my back and I thought that a jolt of electricity went through me as I was pushed up two stairs. I turned around to see who was there, but the only thing I saw was the clothing you'd put on hangers to dry. The heaviest thing there was Roger's camouflage uniform and it was swinging wildly, like someone had given it a whack when he went by. None of the other clothes were moving."

"I knew the house was building up to something, but this is the first time it's gotten physical," I said. "Are you all right?"

"I'm okay," he answered, looking calmer now that he'd told me what'd happened. "You know, I've felt it getting weird around here lately, but after I joined the navy, I decided that we'd all just imagined the strange things that happen here. So even when I saw how Shay was acting, I ignored my own bad feelings about the basement; I wasn't going to let it scare me. I guess whatever it is wanted to teach me a lesson for not believing anymore."

"At least you're okay now," I said. "I don't know what I can do about this house, but I have to think of something. Whatever is here is getting stronger and the odd feelings are coming up more often."

"Dammit!" exclaimed Howard, getting angry, "I had some things to do downstairs. I'm going back down to do them. I'll be darned if I'm going to let something I can't see scare me."

I was surprised he was willing to go back down, but I certainly admired his courage. "If you're going into the basement again, would you please bring my blouse up? It's on the line and I need it for work tomorrow."

"I'm only going as far as the kitchen now," said Howard, shaking his head. "I wouldn't risk the basement again tonight." With that, he went downstairs, but returned again in just a few minutes. He was carrying a glass of milk and some cheese and crackers, not his usual large snack. Standing in my doorway, Howard said, "Now I understand why Heather used to turn on all the lights in the house. As soon as I stepped out into the hall, I had the strong feeling that I was in some kind of danger. I went downstairs anyway, but I turned on every light that I passed. I could hardly stay in the kitchen long enough to pour a glass of milk. I kept having the feeling that something was going to come up the stairs from the basement into the kitchen. But I did force myself to stay there long enough to put some cheese and crackers on a plate. When I was ready to come back upstairs, I found myself turning off each light and then running to the next one, as if I were being chased! I'm not even going out into the hall again tonight."

"Yeah, I always feel safe up here," I said. It was still true. I'd learned long ago that any activity in our upstairs rooms seemed to serve as a warning for us. I was pretty sure the spirit in the window seat had tried to warn Howard not to go downstairs again. More than ever now, I felt certain that the negative spirits would not be allowed to intrude on the territory of the spirits on the second floor. These rooms, with their low ceilings, just

45

felt cozier to me than the rest of the house, so this may have added to my feeling of being protected there.

Howard didn't mention what happened in the basement again, but, within a week, he'd rented an apartment. He borrowed a mattress, a radio, some basic kitchen supplies and a small TV from us and moved immediately, never to sleep in our house again. His family rejoined him a few weeks later.

Not long after Howard moved out, my friend, Maureen, dropped by one night to invite me to dinner. I'd already eaten, so I invited her in for a visit and some refreshment. We hadn't been sitting too long at the dining room table, when the dogs came over and sat at Maureen's feet, facing outwards, as if to protect her from something unseen. She was aware of some of the problems I'd had with the house and was picking up on the strange tension that was developing as we sat there talking. Suddenly, the dogs turned around, and started barking at something under the table. Maureen stood up and said, "I'm leaving right now, want to come?"

"I'm with you," I said, hurrying to the front hall to get my coat. Once in her car, she told me that, just before she stood up, she got a strong impression that she should leave. Then she felt an ice cold hand run up her leg; that was when the dogs started to bark. At the same time, I'd distinctly felt a pair of unseen hands on my shoulders, pushing down as though to keep me in my chair. Maureen drove us to a restaurant, where we stayed for quite a while. As we drove back to the house, a white, odorless mist started to pour out of her car's vents and fog up the windows. There was no smell to this mist and she hadn't had a problem like it before. We cranked down the side windows to try to clear the fog from the windshield, but that didn't help. The closer we got to my house, the harder it was to see out. Maureen was rubbing at the windshield with a cloth, trying to clean it up. At last, she pulled onto a side street, and stopped the car. She used glass cleaner that she had in the car to try to clean the windows inside and out, without success. We sat in the car, talking, and waited. After 10 or 15 minutes, the windows began to clear. She started the engine and we sat for a while; no more fog appeared. Then Maureen drove toward my house again, and again the fog poured out. We were forced to pull over once more.

"It doesn't look like we should be heading to my house, does it." I said.

"No, it certainly doesn't!" Maureen agreed. We waited until most of the fog cleared, and then she said, "Let's try again." Although the window wasn't completely clear, no more fog came out of the vents. We slowly made our way to my house. When we arrived, Roger was just coming in with some friends. I went in with them and noticed that the tension in the house was gone.

The next day, Maureen suggested that I get in touch with Pat, a psychic she knew who lived an hour's drive away, in Des Plaines. Both of us believe that everyone has psychic ability, but that some people have developed their abilities more so than others. We're aware that there are a lot of charlatans in the field, but Maureen had met with Pat many times and was convinced of her legitimacy.

When I called, Pat said, "Come next Saturday afternoon and bring some articles from your home. It doesn't matter what you bring, I just need some things of yours that will help me to pick up psychic impressions." Her voice was very deep and gruff and could easily be mistaken for a man's. I expected her to be a large woman, but when she opened her door, I saw a short woman with steel gray hair. She invited us in and introduced us to a group of women gathered around her living room. Pat explained that she'd invited them to help work on my house. She said that these women all had different types and degrees of psychic abilities. Some were clairvoyant, meaning they could see spirits, some were clairaudiant, meaning they could hear spirits, and some were both.

Pat told me that she used a technique she called "far sight" to work with spirits. She said that holding objects from my home would help her focus on it more clearly, since these things would hold energy in them from my house. (I have since learned that the U.S. military has spent years experimenting with this phenomenon, and refer to it as "remote viewing.")

As Pat passed around the objects that I'd brought, she asked the other psychics to concentrate on what was so frightening in my basement. Each person began to describe what she saw and felt in my basement. I was startled at the detail they provided about the layout of my basement. Together, they came up with the impression of a farmer who had waited until his death for his son to return from the army. His son had been missing in action from some long-ago conflict, but the old man never gave up hope that he would return. One day, as the old man went down the stairs of his root cellar, with his dog following him, he tripped and fell. He died at the foot of the stairs from a heart attack. His dog stayed by him, howling in distress.

"Could this be the dog Roger and I heard howling in the basement late one night?" I wondered. I listened as they pieced the story together. They decided that the man checked each newcomer to the house in the hope that his son had returned. He'd get angry that none of the people who came into the basement was his son. He regarded all of us as intruders who got in the way of his son's homecoming.

Then Pat spoke aloud to the man's spirit, explaining that he was dead and had to move into the light. She promised him that he could return if he wanted to. Her promise alarmed me, but Pat explained, "I've done this many times. The invitation to return gives the spirit the confidence to seek the light. Once a spirit has been to the light, it's no longer troubled and won't cause any more distress. Sometimes a spirit returns to help those who've helped him." She asked everyone in the room to imagine that the man's spirit had gone to a park in the middle of town, where he met up with his son and the rest of his family at a gazebo. Pat called on a spirit she called Sister Anna and asked her to help the unhappy soul to find his way, and then Pat instructed his spirit to go with his family towards Sister Anna and the light of God.

Once his spirit was gone, she had everyone imagine that a purifying smoke was filling my house, starting from the basement and moving up through every room until it reached the roof. We sat quietly, at first, concentrating on this visualization. Then individuals in the group began to spontaneously explain what they were seeing as they watched the smoke moving from the basement to the attic. I was again amazed at how accurately some of them described various rooms. None of them lived anywhere near me and, except for Maureen, they hadn't been in my house.

"Now," said Pat, "you shouldn't have any more trouble with your basement. But you're a helpful person, so you can expect to attract lost souls all your life. Moving won't help. I'm not even sure if the farmer actually died on your land or if he somehow found you."

This was not very reassuring news to me. I went home that day wanting to believe that the basement problem was solved, but it was months before I was really sure of it. At first, I thought that the peace in the

49

basement was merely a lull in activity. I remained on guard, but when the atmosphere grew tense in the house again, and the basement remained benign, I finally believed that Pat had solved my main problem. Before the year was out, however, I had to call on her to help me with spirits in other parts of the house.

Late one Saturday afternoon in November of 1992, Bill and I were upstairs when we heard someone come into the house. The footsteps were heavy as the visitor walked from room to room on the main floor. Since I was about to step into the shower, I asked Bill to see who was there.

"It could be Roger," I said; "although, the footsteps are heavy enough to be Howard." Bill went down to greet our visitor, but returned almost immediately, with a puzzled look on his face.

"There was no one there, and no car in the driveway," he said. "But I could've sworn I heard someone unlock the front door and come in."

"I thought so, too," I agreed. "Oh well, chalk it up to the other family, I guess. They've been quiet for a while." With that, I stepped into the tub and started my shower. But while I was showering, I could hear the loud noises again. This time, they were coming from the main floor bathroom. That bathroom has a door that slides into place. It was being repeatedly slammed shut and then thrown open. "What on earth is going on?" I wondered. Sound from the main floor seldom carried to the second storey, and it certainly wouldn't be heard in the upstairs bathroom when water was running. I finished showering in a hurry and dried off quickly. "There'd better be someone down there now, or I'm really going to be upset," I called out to Bill as I wrapped my hair in a towel. "Did you hear that racket?"

"Yes, I did. I kept expecting Howard or Roger to come up and say hello," said Bill; then he paused before adding, "The really odd thing is that the dogs haven't made a sound since all the noise started. They'd normally be barking up a storm by now if they'd heard anyone walking around. I'm going down to check."

"Wait for me," I said, doing up my bathrobe as I ran after him. When we reached the foot of the stairs, we saw that the front door was still locked. "Most of the noise seemed to come from the bathroom down here," I said.

"That's what it sounded like to me, too," said Bill. When we reached the bathroom, the door was open. "Nobody's here," he said. He looked down each side of the hall. "The library and bedroom doors are shut, just the way I left them," he added. He turned left, and I followed him down the narrow hall to the library. After opening the door, he stepped inside and looked around. I remained in the hall. "Nothing here," he declared. With that, he left the library and closed the door behind him. I stepped aside, so he could go to the other end of the hall and check out the spare bedroom. As he opened the door and stepped inside, he had already begun to speak. "Nothing h...Oh!"

"'Oh'? What do you mean by 'Oh'?" I demanded, being careful to stay in the hall. I had heard and felt many strange things in the house over the years, but I wasn't volunteering to rush into them headlong. Bill looked towards the left corner, and then turned his gaze back to the center of the room.

"There's something in the corner of the room, all huddled up," he said, quietly. "I can't make out a distinguishing shape, it's just some kind of blob, but it has eyes." He turned in the direction of the creature and then turned his head back again. "I can see him with my peripheral vision, but not when I try to look directly at him. You know; the way it was with Dick Tracy."

"Could it be Dick Tracy?" I asked. At least I knew that one was harmless.

"Somehow, I don't think so," Bill said. "This one doesn't have his distinctive features. Just the eyes are showing. He only seems to come up to about my waist."

"Could it be the Track Star?" I asked, wanting this to be another of the 'harmless' spirits we'd seen in the past.

"I don't know. Let's see," he said. He raised his voice and asked, "Are you the little boy who runs through our house?" Then Bill said to me, "I don't know what I'm expecting him to say, but it never hurts to try." After a few quiet moments, Bill spoke to me again. "Whatever it is, it's fading...Now it's gone." Bill and I went into the living room to discuss what had just taken place. Try as we might, we were unable to come up with a rational explanation for what had happened.

"I love this house, but I don't think I can stay here if we don't find a solution to this problem," I said, at last. "So far, whenever you've been out of town, one of the kids has been living here, or we've had house guests. I can't imagine staying here alone, for days on end, when the house is in an uproar."

"How about inviting your friend, Maureen, or one of the kids over when I'm away?" Bill suggested. "Or maybe, you could go and stay with one of them, or rent a room in a hotel."

"I won't upset anyone else's routine just because we have a problem here," I replied. "And as for staying in a hotel, what would I do with the dogs? Anyway, I'd feel silly being driven out of my own house every time you had to take a trip." We thought about this for a while and then I remembered the help Pat had been in getting rid of our basement problem. "I think I'll call

Maureen and get Pat's phone number," I said, already dialing the phone. "Maybe Pat can help with this new spirit."

Maureen answered the phone right away. As it happened, she had Pat on the other line. Through Maureen, I was able to relay what had happened that day. Pat wanted to know if the spirit had reappeared. Bill went back to the bedroom and checked. Sure enough, it was back. Maureen informed Pat of this and then returned to the line with me to say, "Pat said she'll try to work on your house from her own home tonight. If that doesn't work, you can arrange to go to her house one day next week."

While Bill and I waited to hear from Pat, Roger stopped in for a moment on his way to a movie. We told him what'd been going on and that Pat was going to try to help us. "I can't stay and argue the point, because Jenn is waiting in the car," Roger said, "but, I don't think you should let a psychic get involved. She probably can't do anything for you from her house, anyway. And, if she does contact the spirit, she might make things worse."

"We'll take our chances and let Pat try," I said. "Something has to be done to make this house livable again." Just then, the phone rang. It was Pat. She'd been able to contact the spirit of a man who believed our house was his.

"I used 'far sight' to get into your house and found myself sitting in a rocking chair at the head of some stairs," she said. "There was a window seat on my left and the spirit of the man who'd been making all the racket appeared before me, crouching on the stairs. He wore a black cloak with a large collar that he held close to his face to hide his identity. When he finally stood up, I could see that he was quite tall, but he'd been crouching to hide from everyone. At first, he attempted to intimidate me with his height and his anger, he even tried to upset the rocker I was sitting in; but I've had years of dealing with spirits and they don't frighten me anymore."

"Aren't you afraid of being hurt by any of them?" I asked, remembering how they'd been able to touch some of us physically.

"I've learned," she replied, "that, as long as I have faith in God, and ask for his protection before I begin to work with the spirits, nothing they do can harm me. They are no more powerful than we are. You have to treat them as you would a person who has come into your home. If someone staying with you went into rooms you didn't want them to, or made a lot of noise, or tried to push you around, you would tell them to shape up or leave. You can do the same with the spirits, as long as you believe that you can."

"So what happened when you wouldn't let him scare you?" I asked.

"At first, he was surprised," Pat said. "Then, he decided to calm down and talk to me. He said he'd made all the noise because he was angry, but he didn't know why. When I told him he was dead, he said he knew that. I asked him why he didn't go to the light so he could be with God, but he was afraid to move on. He was sure he was going to Hell. It took quite a while for me to convince him that he wouldn't. I had to call on some of my spirit guides to show him the way."

"What are spirit guides?" I asked.

"Spirit guides are our teachers. They can come to us at any time and leave us when we no longer need them. At each stage in our lives, we have different lessons to learn. At school, we wouldn't expect an English teacher to teach us algebra. That's why, for different spiritual tasks, we have different spirit guides available to us. They can help us even if we're not aware of their existence. For instance, when we feel that we are acting on our intuition, we are often acting on advice from one of our spirit guides. We can even ask them directly to help us. When I want help leading a lost spirit to the light, I call on Sister Anna. She is a spirit guide whose role is to help troubled spirits."

Now that I understood that, I wanted to know more about the spirit Pat had just sent to the light. "Why was that spirit so afraid? Did he tell you his name or why he thought he'd go to Hell?" I asked.

"No, he didn't," Pat replied. "It took so much energy just to try to convince him to leave, that I didn't think to ask for details. After he left, his cloak hung in the air on its own for a few seconds, dark and evil looking. Then it disintegrated and the pieces just vanished."

While Pat and I were talking, Bill went into the bedroom and confirmed that the spirit had indeed disappeared. "Bill says it's gone, but now I need to know what to do the next time this happens. If it keeps up, I'm afraid we'll have to move."

"There's no point in moving, Sandra," Pat said. "You'll only take them with you. You attract spirits who need help. I'll try to get together with you soon and show you how to work with them. In the meantime, remember that that's your house and the spirits are simply guests in it. You can insist that they behave, because they can't really be there without your permission."

"Somebody should've told that to the spirit we once had in the basement," I said. I was having a hard time believing that we could so easily affect the spirit world. "What about evil spirits?"

"I don't believe in evil spirits," she said firmly. "Some of them are very angry or afraid, so they can make you feel uncomfortable. If you really feel you need help, imagine a white light around you that will represent God's protection. Spirits communicate on thought level, after all. If you bring God into the situation, how can anything harm you?"

"Well, I'll try it next time," I said. "We have enough activity in this house, I'll probably get the chance to test your theory soon."

"That reminds me. After I'd helped the man in the cloak, some other spirits came forward. Did you know you had some Civil War soldiers there?" she asked.

"I knew we had one," I replied.

"No," she said, "there were several. They'd been killed in battle. In their panic, they weren't aware that they were dead. Once I got through to them that they didn't have to run from the enemy anymore, they went gratefully into the light. Then a little blonde-haired boy appeared. He said he liked your house because there were children and toys to play with. Did you know about him?"

"Oh yes," I replied. "I've even seen him once. He must be the one who sets off the kids' musical toys."

"Well," said Pat, "I asked him if he wanted to go to Heaven and play with the other little children. I promised him he could come back if he wanted to. He agreed to go but first he had to get his teddy bear. Then, he knelt down and started to pull on something as though it were stuck. Eventually, he pulled out a cinnamon colored teddy bear with the old fashioned, long cloth snout instead of the button nose. Once he had that, he went happily off to the light with the spirit guides."

We continued to talk for a while and Pat explained that she'd become interested in the spirit world after her father died in 1948. Suddenly, strange things started happening around the house, and she could feel his presence. She'd always been aware she was psychic, but this new spirit activity made Pat more determined to read up on the subject and hone her capabilities. "I use far sight to get into the spirit world and work with troubled spirits and those waiting to help them on the other side. I really think anyone can learn to do this if they really want to help troubled souls. I begin by saying a prayer to make sure that what I do is only for the good of all. I can also tune in on a person who is living at a distance, to do a reading for them for instance. But I would never tune into someone without that person's permission."

At the end of the conversation, Pat agreed to come to my house in the spring, when the weather was more predictable. Once off the phone, I reported everything she'd said about our house to my husband. "The house is going to feel kind of empty if she sent off that many members of our other family," he said. "While you were talking to Pat, Roger came rushing back in and ran up the stairs. When he came down, he told me that he and Jennifer saw the face of an old woman, with white hair pulled back, staring out of the window on the second floor. But when he went upstairs, there was no one on the window seat." Bill paused, and then added "He's really worried about us asking anyone to mess with our house."

"Well, if it means getting rid of some of the scary spirits, I'm glad Pat's around to do it," I said. After that, Bill and I agreed to change the subject.

"I got rid of a lot of junk in the attic while you were out today," Bill said. "Then I reorganized the rest of it. Your old technical books are at the very front in three boxes so you can get to them easily. Come upstairs and I'll show you." I was glad for this distraction, so we went up, and he attempted to open the attic door. It was stuck again, as it often was. The bottom of the door moved easily, but the top remained firmly in place. He hauled on the door until, finally, it opened. Bill stepped inside, and turned on the light. There, on top of a box of my technical books, lay a cinnamon brown teddy bear with a long, cloth snout. "I don't know where that came from!" Bill said in surprise. "There were no stuffed toys in here when I cleaned it out today." This bear was from Heather's stuffed toy collection that she'd disposed of years before.

Maureen took the bear to Pat's house the following week, and was told that it looked exactly like the teddy bear the little boy had carried with him to the light.

In the spring of 1993, Pat came to my house for a visit. By that time, I was very happy and comfortable in my home. There was still a lot of spirit activity, but it was not threatening; it seemed natural.

Pat went through each room, and then, as we sat in the living room, she said, "The spirit of an old woman is standing in front of us. Do you see her?"

"No," I said, "but I can feel her presence."

"She has long white hair which she has pulled back and she's wearing an old fashioned purple dress." Pat paused for a moment and then went on. "Apparently, she sits in your upstairs hall window seat and looks out over the grave of her young daughter."

"I wonder if she's the one Roger saw in our window the night you cleared our house of spirits?" I said. Then something else, more startling, occurred to me. "You know, Pat," I said, "shortly after we moved into our house, a patch of grass on the front lawn died out under our white pine tree. No matter what we tried, from fertilizing to reseeding with shade grass, nothing would stay long on that spot. We soon realized that the bare patch resembled the shape of a child's small coffin.

We kidded each other about this over the years. But now, it seems, the shape of that patch was not a coincidence."

"Apparently, she's been trying to get through to you for a long time. Did she ever tell you her name?" asked Pat.

"No," I said.

"Let's see if she'll tell us now," said Pat. We sat there in silence for a few short moments before the name "Agatha" was spoken clearly in my head. I decided not to speak up. I wanted to see if Pat would hear it, too.

"I'm getting 'Agatha'," she said at last.

"So did I!" I said, excited that I'd been able to receive this information just by asking. What were the odds that we'd both come up with such an uncommon name together, purely by chance?

Then Pat continued, "She's a woman with a very sad story, and she wants you to tell it."

"How on earth could I do that?" I asked. "I just found out her name now, after all this time. It would take me years to get her story, assuming I got it right."

"She can't leave until her story's been told, and she expects you to tell it," Pat insisted. "Each day, sit on the stairs with a pen and pad ready. Tell Agatha you've come to write her story; then write down whatever comes into your mind. It will take time, but you'll be amazed at how accurate it is. Just don't second guess the words that come into your mind. And once you get started, you'll be able to write her story anywhere in the house."

I agreed to try. That night, after supper, I sat on the stairs and said, aloud, "I'm here to write your story, Agatha." Then I closed my eyes to relax and wait. The vision of a woman's head and shoulders came in to my mind, and the following words started to flow, "My name is Agatha Wilson. I am 49 years old..."

SECTION 2

AGATHA'S JOURNEY THROUGH SPACE

Chapter 3

Agatha Wilson was born in Ireland in 1784. Her mother had been to Boston in her youth to work as an indentured servant. This was the way in which many of the Irish were able to afford to go to the New World and seek their fortune. Once they had fulfilled their agreed-upon time of servitude, they were free to live as they wished. Agatha's mother had had a change of heart, however. When her indenture was completed, she chose to return to Ireland to marry her childhood sweetheart.

Agatha, on the other hand, had no particular interest in traveling or romance. She loved living in Ireland, and was not made discontent by her mother's entertaining stories of life in America. Like her mother, Agatha was short, with red hair and hazel eyes; but, while her mother had a quick wit and hot temper, she had her father's reserved manner. She took each day as it came, helping with the chores and learning to do the delicate embroidery on the linens that every young woman prepared for the day she would set up her own household. On rare occasions, when she felt she must have her own way, Agatha quietly dug in her heels and worked to make events turn out as she wanted them.

For example, when Agatha was 19, the local tavern owner, Mr. McGinness, began to court her. At first, he made a point of stopping to talk to her family after church. He was always careful to direct some of his comments and questions to Agatha so that she wouldn't wander off to talk to her friends. Mr.

McGinness was a widower and twice her age, so at first she thought his interest was in chatting with her parents. As time went on, he developed the habit of stopping by their home late on Sunday afternoons when he was sure to be invited to stay for supper. It became clear to everyone that Mr. McGinness was interested in Agatha as a potential wife for him and mother to his four young children. His first wife had died in childbirth and his children were now living with his sister and her husband in the next county. Mr. McGinness made a good living and was considered by all to be a very decent man and a good catch for any young woman. Agatha, however, was not prepared to settle down yet. She liked the freedom to come and go as she pleased, once her chores were done. While some girls married at her age, usually to older men, most young men and women waited until they were in their middle or late twenties to wed.

Although Agatha's parents would certainly have approved of her marrying a man like Mr. McGinness, and arranged marriages were more the rule at that time, theirs had been a love match. They didn't want to force anything different on their daughter. Her mother, however, did point out the man's fine qualities and the good life Agatha could have as his wife.

At first, she pretended not to understand Mr. McGinness' interest in her. She avoided all of his efforts to get her to spend any time alone with him. When he invited her to go for a walk one Sunday afternoon, Agatha, who truly loved long country walks, said she had turned her ankle and suggested he walk with her father while she helped her mother prepare dinner. During the walk, Mr. McGinness made his feelings crystal clear to her father and appealed for his help in persuading her to consider marriage.

"Shame on you for lying to that good man," her mother chided, as they prepared dinner. "Now you must be sure to favor your foot all night or he will be embarrassed." Agatha realized then that she should have said she had a headache instead, since that would not have required such an elaborate charade. That night, during dinner, Agatha's mother couldn't resist teasing her daughter by having her get up frequently to fetch something for the table. By the end of the evening, the young woman resolved to find a better solution to the problem of Mr. McGinness.

As time went on, many of the villagers began teasing Agatha about setting her wedding date, but she refused to even discuss the topic of marriage with her family and friends. Instead, she sought out the company of a village woman who was a widow in her mid thirties. Agatha befriended this woman and began inviting her and her two children to Sunday dinner. She would spend much of the evening playing with the youngsters while everyone else was involved in pleasant conversation. Mr. McGinness understood what was being done and turned his attentions where they'd do the most good. By year's end, there was a wedding. Six children now had two parents, and Agatha still had her freedom.

The years passed by and, one by one, all of Agatha's childhood friends married. It seemed she'd valued her freedom for too long; her parents were resigned to her staying with them forever. Agatha was their only living child and they'd hoped one day she'd be married and provide them with many grandchildren. She watched as her friends became mothers, and she noticed that each of these women established her own style for running the household. Agatha understood then that there was a form of independence even in marriage. A feeling of emptiness grew within her. When she saw her friends with their new babies, she realized how much she wanted a family of her own. But there was no use complaining; Agatha had made her own choices, and life with her parents was filled with the friendly chatter of their many visitors.

Sometimes friends and neighbors would gather in Agatha's home and listen to her mother's stories of life in Boston. America seemed to be a place full of opportunities for people who were willing to work hard and take chances. One bachelor, who used to come regularly to the house, asked many questions about life in America. His own mother had worked on the estate of a wealthy land owner and had married another servant, an Englishman who insisted that their son be raised in the Protestant faith. Outwardly, he was, but his mother secretly tutored him in her Catholic religion. When he grew older, he worked in the fields, far from the disapproving eyes of his father, who regretted marrying an Irish woman. When his mother died, he left the estate, looking for a place to live where he would feel welcome and could practice his faith more openly. He arrived at Agatha's village and soon found work as a farm hand. On Sundays he would listen to the stories of America and dream about a country where true religious freedom existed, and a man could own his own house and land.

At 32, he was eager to embark on his own adventure, but wanted a good Irish wife to take with him. He soon took notice of Agatha and began to spend time with her. After a brief courtship, he proposed. She didn't love him, but he seemed a decent sort of person who was popular with the people from their village. By now, Agatha was 36 years old. She realized that she must marry soon if she was ever to have children of her own. As for his desire to move to America, Agatha

66

realized it would be years before they could save enough money for the trip. There was a good possibility that he would change his mind and decide to stay. On the other hand, she didn't have many years or choices left if she wanted to have a family of her own. Being a practical person, she accepted his proposal. They married a few months later and moved in with Agatha's parents to save money for the trip to America.

Agatha was pleased that she was still living with her parents, for she knew the day might soon come when she would leave them forever. Her parents lived in a house they'd built, but they didn't own the land they lived on. They leased their land in a "leases for lives" system, whereby a person could rent land that would stay in the family as long as that person or two other people named on the lease lived. If one or two of the people on the list died, additional people could be added to the lease for a fee, provided the landlord agreed. Agatha's father had leased the land when she was a baby. He'd named himself, his wife, and Agatha as the three lease holders. Most of the land in the area was held by a few landowners, but it was being divided into smaller parcels by the lease holders. All of her life, Agatha had expected to be given the use of a portion of her father's farm to work with her husband when she married. Eventually, she would inherit her parents' house and would be able to add the names of her husband and one child to the lease. Now, however, she was married to a man who made it clear that he wouldn't give up on his plans to emigrate. There was no need to divide up the land since her husband had no interest in it.

Shortly after Agatha married, her family's landlord approached all of his tenants with an offer to buy back their leases in return for passage to America. He hadn't been making much money on the leases and hoped to reclaim the land to use for grazing. It was his belief that the money he could make raising livestock was well worth the emigration expenses. The landlord intended to regain all of the land eventually; he made it clear that he wouldn't allow any new people to be added to the lease as the older leaseholders died.

Agatha's parents turned him down. They felt they were much too old to leave all that was familiar to them and start again in a new country. But to Agatha, this was an opportunity for her own new family to make a good start. If she accepted the offer, the money they'd planned to save for their passage on board ship could be used instead for the purchase of land and building materials in America. She approached the landlord and asked him to let her wait a few years while she and her husband saved what they needed for their new start. Not knowing how many children she might have by the time they were ready to leave, she also stipulated that the landlord would have to pay the passage for any children she might have by the time she and her husband were ready to emigrate. As Agatha further pointed out, she was young enough to hold the land for a long time if he didn't let her out of the lease on her terms, so he agreed.

Agatha's husband was overjoyed with the deal she'd struck and very impressed with her business sense. Agatha, however, was of two minds about what she'd accomplished. It was true that this was the only way her husband could realize his dream of making a fresh start in America; but, since the passage back to Ireland would be too expensive, they could never return. She also knew that her parents would never be able to join them or visit them in America. Her mother had a heart problem now and could not make such a journey.

Not long after the deal was made, Agatha became pregnant. It pleased her to know that her parents would have their grandchild with them for a few years.

When the time came to give birth to her baby, Agatha stayed at home where she was assisted by her mother and a midwife. The men, being of no use in the birthing process, went to the local pub to await the news. Women from the village stopped by periodically to check on Agatha's progress. When at last her son was born, one of the local boys was sent to the pub to fetch Father and Grandfather. The baby, whom they christened Daniel David Wilson, had his father's black hair and blue eyes.

She hadn't realized how frightening it could be to take on the responsibility for such a tiny being, but her mother reassured her that such nervousness was natural. With her mother's encouragement, Agatha learned to trust her own maternal instincts. For a little while, Agatha and her husband felt the joy of new parenthood. To them, no other baby had ever been as beautiful or bright as their Daniel. They viewed his every move with wonder and dreamed about the opportunities he'd have in America one day. Then, without warning, Daniel developed a fever that could not be controlled. Within a week he was dead. He was two months old.

Agatha and her mother bathed the infant and dressed him in white for his funeral. He was laid out in a small coffin built by his grandfather. Friends and neighbors gathered in the main room of the house for the wake that night. The next day, they all gathered in the church for the funeral and then stood in the church graveyard as the priest sprinkled earth onto the small coffin. Agatha accepted the condolences of their friends quietly, with a stoicism born of shock. She even comforted her husband who cried as the mood took him over the loss of their son. She herself did not cry. Finally, when weeks had gone by with no tears, Agatha's mother sent the men out of the house and sat Agatha down to talk about her loss. At first, Agatha resisted her mother's attempts but her mother wouldn't stop talking about Daniel. "He was a sweet baby that we were blessed to have in our lives," said her mother. "You must not pretend that we never had that gift from God."

"How could God give us Daniel and then snatch him back so soon?" Agatha asked bitterly.

"Sometimes God takes the wee ones to be with him. You are our only child although I bore five children. We should all be grateful for the time God let us have Daniel. Your baby is in heaven now and has escaped the suffering that we all have to endure as we grow older," her mother said softly.

"But what of me?" demanded Agatha, finally near tears. "I am not so young that I can keep having babies, hoping that God will let me keep one!"

"Do not be angry with God!" Agatha's mother said sharply, then more calmly she added, "God is merciful and will surely grant you another baby in His own time. You must speak to the priest about these doubts when you go to confession. Now, we should pray together that God will bless you and your husband with more children."

Agatha did as her mother told her. She let go of her anger and let the tears come to wash away the grief. Within a year, at age 38, she gave birth to Sarah, a blond-haired, blue-eyed baby who was healthy and brought much joy to the household. Agatha lavished love and attention on her daughter, taking great pride in each new step of the baby's growth. As Sarah grew older, Agatha took her on walks through the countryside, pointing out the wonders of nature to her little girl. Although Agatha and her husband would have liked to have a large family, they were happy with Sarah, and accepted her as God's blessing to them when Agatha failed to have any more children.

For six years after Sarah's birth, they continued to live with Agatha's parents until at last they had enough money to go to America. During that time people continued to gather at the house to visit, but the visits were fewer and didn't last as long. Many of the older villagers, including Agatha's mother, were in failing health and didn't stay up late anymore. Most of the young people who used to visit had moved to America. There simply was not enough land for everyone to work. The older generation chose to stay in Ireland; the sea voyage to America, and a new life with new ways, were more than they cared to take on. Sadly, Agatha knew that her time with her parents, in the country that she loved, was drawing to a close. She began the painful process of sorting through their belongings for what they could take and what they must leave behind.

As the day to depart drew closer, Agatha began to have misgivings about moving to a country so far away. One evening, as she was helping her mother prepare dinner, Agatha began to cry. "Oh Mother, I don't want to leave. Why can't we stay here in the safety and comfort of our family home? Why does my husband have to take us so far away?"

Agatha's mother sat her gently down at the table. "This is not like you, Agatha," she said. "As the wife you must be calm. Your family will depend upon your strength to endure in the new country. The man may be head of the family, but it is the woman who must hold it all together. Remember, your duty is to help your husband build a new home in America and to teach your daughter the duties of a young woman as she grows up."

"I shall miss you, Mother," said Agatha, regaining control of her emotions. She knew her mother was right. She'd married knowing her husband wanted to emigrate, now she must face this move with dignity.

"You and your family will always be in my heart and in my prayers," her mother said softly as they rose from the table. She turned her back on Agatha and bent over the cooking pot, struggling to get her own emotions under control. Agatha could see what was happening, so she waited. If she spoke now, her mother's own composure might break. It was important to both of them that this not happen. After a few moments, Agatha's mother took a deep breath and, without looking back at her daughter, said, "Now come, we must get dinner ready before the men come home."

With that, the women resumed their cooking. As they worked, Agatha resolved to stop thinking of herself and giving in to her fears. She would go with her husband to America and make a good home for her family, no matter what difficulties lay ahead.

Chapter 4

In 1828, Agatha set sail with her husband and daughter for New York. Her husband was a dreamer who was eager to buy a home for his family, something they could never afford to do in Ireland. He thought that land was cheap in America and that he would soon be able to buy, or build, a home in New York. Once there, he was appalled to discover how much it would cost just to rent some rooms in someone else's house. The only jobs he could find didn't pay well and most of his savings had been spent on outfitting their small apartment with furniture and other necessities. He realized his dream of being a landowner would die unless a miracle occurred.

Agatha helped out by taking in laundry for some of the well-to-do families. She was also able to get work as a seamstress, but this still didn't bring in enough money for them to better themselves. Agatha accepted this; it was only important to her that they have enough to eat and a place to stay. As long as her family was healthy, she was content. Her husband, on the other hand, grew more and more restless and out of sorts, unable to accept the fact that his dream was impossible. He resented the long hours they had to work just to keep food on the table. How he wished they'd never left Ireland!

Then one day, during their second winter in New York, he came home all excited. He'd heard that land was being given to people who wanted to settle in California. Some men where he worked were organizing an expedition of people who were willing to brave the elements, Indians, and all sorts of unknown dangers to travel to California and claim the land. His spirits rose. He could talk of nothing else.

The journey to the Mexican territory of California could take at least six months. Because of this, those who signed up for the wagon train were warned to be ready to go by the first of May. There was little time to decide, he told Agatha. They were expected to sell their excess belongings and pack the rest, with care, in preparation for the long journey.

At first Agatha resisted her husband's new dream. She knew she was strong enough to face the hardships of such an undertaking, but was concerned about the safety and well-being of young Sarah. Agatha's husband, however, would not give up on this opportunity. He did not believe it could be that dangerous because so many people would be traveling together. He would not give Agatha any peace until finally she agreed to meet the men who would lead the expedition.

Chapter 5

The leaders of the expedition were two brothers,
Robert and Joseph Colins, bachelors who'd grown up in
an Irish working class neighborhood in New York City.
Robert had dreams of becoming an important man, a
leader in the community. He knew he wasn't meant to
be a factory worker. He was a tall, dark-haired man of
26; but with a receding hairline and a bit of a paunch,
most people thought he was 40. He did not correct this
impression since it lent him a certain amount of respect
amongst the other workers. This illusion of age, coupled
with his natural air of authority, enabled him to be
promoted quickly to the position of factory foreman.
Robert's younger brother, Joseph, was 24, tall and
slender, with curly brown hair. Joseph was content to
work in the factory where his brother was foreman. He
had no particular ambitions for himself; his dreams were
for Robert's success. When they were children, Joseph
would listen as Robert made up stories of one day
owning his own company, and making Joseph his
partner so they could work together.

After years of working effectively as a foreman,
saving his money, and looking for better opportunities,
Robert realized his dreams would never be fulfilled in
New York City. There were definite class lines that he
couldn't break through. The earliest Irish immigrants
had been well-to-do people who were prepared to give up
their old ways and adapt to the values of the New World
inhabitants. They had done well for themselves, but
were not so willing to help the newcomers from Ireland

who tended to be poor, and who were not so inclined to work long hard hours for meager wages. These rural men were used to seasonal labor and were more inclined to interrupt their work for social events. Robert often found that recent Irish immigrants seeking employment at the factory thought nothing of taking time off to celebrate weddings, for instance. They didn't understand the work ethic in their new homeland. With a large labor force to choose from, Robert would fire those who failed to show up for work due to family illness and other distractions. Those employees who did remain on the job were not rewarded with great increases in pay or chances to move into management, but Robert knew they were ambitious. As for his own future, he could see that he'd risen as far as he could in the city. Being a member of the Irish working class, he now faced the stigma attached to the Irish working poor as people unworthy of promotion. He decided he'd either have to give up his dream or leave New York.

Robert began to follow newspaper accounts of the adventures of people who'd moved out west. He obtained additional information about these adventures when he and Joseph visited the local tavern. Robert would drink, but not too much. His purpose was to gather information about the West. He'd start up a conversation about what life must be like on the frontier and then listen carefully as men talked about letters they'd received from relatives who'd moved to Illinois, Mississippi, and the Mexican territory of Texas. Robert also heard stories about the role of the soldiers in the forts.

Soldiers had to keep the peace between the settlers and the Indians throughout the West. With so much territory to protect, they couldn't be expected to accompany each expedition. Robert thought a wise expedition leader would check with the soldiers at the forts along the way to see if there was any danger from the Indians in that area. He also learned that the size of the expeditions to the west could vary greatly. Some people set out in small groups, consisting of one or two families; others organized much larger groups made up of 16 to 20 families and other individuals who tagged along. From what Robert heard, it seemed that a larger group, though harder to lead, had a better chance of surviving the elements and attacks from hostile Indians.

Robert began to dream about leading a large group of families to homesteads in the new west. He wanted the challenge of going beyond the tame areas near the forts. He saw himself, like Moses, leading the people to a new promised land. Then Robert heard about California. Although it was in Mexican territory, Americans had been allowed to settle there. It was a place full of variety and adventure, with mountains, a desert, and an ocean. He had only to pick his destination and recruit some men with a desire for more than factory work in their hearts.

Joseph listened to his brother's ideas and agreed to help with the recruiting. Since Robert was a foreman at the factory, he had to be careful not to talk too much about the expedition at work. He told Joseph to find out which men were interested in such an undertaking. Over the course of the next month, nearly 50 men from the factory and the neighborhood said they were interested in an expedition. Robert and Joseph then approached these men and began the intensive job of truly selling them on such a move. They had to make the idea of finally owning their own homestead sound exciting enough to offset the danger and expense of the expedition. Robert had carefully planned the route, and he described this in detail to make the project sound possible and desirable.

He'd decided they must all travel by boat from New York, along the Hudson River to the Erie Canal, where a barge would take them to Buffalo. He knew that, before the canal was built, the overland trip from New York to Buffalo took 20 days. It also cost a great deal of money in tolls, placed at intervals along the road, for wagons and livestock. By using the new Erie Canal, he discovered, they could make the trip to the Great Lakes in 8 days and pay one toll based on the weight of the goods they were bringing with them. Then, from Buffalo, they could go by boat through the Great Lakes to Chicago, where they could purchase wagons and the necessary supplies for the overland trip. The group would then travel by land from Chicago to Independence, Missouri where they'd pick up the Santa Fe Trail to Santa Fe, Mexico. Finally, from Santa Fe, they would follow the Old Spanish Trail through California, until they found a good place to settle near Los Angeles.

His careful planning of the route and timing of the expedition demonstrated that he wanted to save both time and money for the people who would make the journey. It sounded possible; even exciting. Men with no hope of improving their lives in New York became enthused by Robert's vision of a future unfettered by working class restrictions on their lives. When the time came for the expedition to begin, twenty of the fifty men were able to afford the trip and accept the risk to their families. Agatha's husband was among them, but he hadn't been able to convince her that the move was better than staying in New York.

Chapter 6

Agatha's husband brought the Colins brothers to his apartment one Sunday in a final effort to convince her that the trip to California was worthwhile. They went into the kitchen where Agatha was brewing a pot of tea. The men stood facing her, waiting for her to notice them. Agatha turned and viewed the men with skepticism. "So, you have been able to convince my husband that this is a wonderful adventure he shouldn't miss; that there is land out there for everyone who makes the trip. What makes you think this is so?" she asked, her arms folded firmly across her chest. She addressed her comments to Robert Colins, who had the bearing of a leader and was clearly the prime mover in this enterprise.

"Your husband shares our dream of owning his own home and a piece of land to farm, Mrs. Wilson," said Robert in a conciliatory tone. He nodded in his brother's direction and added, "My brother Joseph and I have always believed that a man should be his own landlord. There should be room to grow your own food, raise cattle or keep chickens, if you like. As hard as we've worked, we know that we can never afford our own home in New York. The thought of marrying and starting a family here is unacceptable. Your husband and all the men who are bringing their families on this trip know this could be their last chance to find land they can afford."

"But why now?" asked Agatha. "California is so far away and my husband tells me this will be the first large group to try it. Why not wait and let others go first? Let them blaze the trail so that it will be safer and easier for us." Agatha laid the teacups on the table and gestured for the men to sit down.

"Soon, hundreds of families will decide to risk the trip to California and the land will be gone," said Robert. As the other two men sat down, Robert stood with his hands resting on the back of his chair and, leaning forward for emphasis, said, "Now is the time to start out while there is good land to choose from." Standing straight again, Robert looked around the room at Agatha and her husband, and said, "Right now your family is healthy and you still have a little money set aside. While you wait here for a better time to make the trip, your money will go to increased rent; your resolve to make the move will disappear as you work harder and longer to pay for food and lodging."

Robert sat down at the kitchen table with Agatha's husband and Joseph while she poured the tea. Agatha thought about these arguments as she sipped at the hot brew in her cup. Then Joseph spoke up. "If you're worried about us knowing the way, Mrs. Wilson, you should know that my brother has worked hard establishing the route we will take. For instance, now that the Erie Canal is open, we can save a lot of time and money using it instead of starting out with the wagons from here. Hunters and map makers and some earlier settlers have created trails we can follow. There may not be a lot of roads yet, but most of the trails are well marked and we will encounter other settlements along the way. At these settlements, we can refurbish our supplies and get the latest information on the route we are following. If any members of our expedition should decide they don't want to keep going to California, they can safely stop at one of these settlements."

"This adventure may be fine for you. Two young men without families can afford to take risks, but we have Sarah to think of. If anything happens to us, what will become of her?" demanded Agatha.

"What will become of her if you stay here, Mrs. Wilson?" Robert asked quietly. "I don't want a family yet. The thought of raising children here, to work as hard, or harder, than I do and not own any property to call their own is not one of my dreams. Do you really want Sarah to spend her life doing other people's laundry, making beautiful clothes for other women and children, or cleaning other people's houses? Don't you want her to have room and time to play and grow on your own land? When Sarah grows up, she may marry a farmer or a store owner. That could never happen here."

Agatha could see the wisdom in Robert's arguments and Joseph had demonstrated that they had planned the best route. She looked over at her husband who was nodding in agreement to Robert's argument about the improvement such a move would make for Sarah. She knew that moving to New York had been a shock to her husband. It was nothing like his dream and he obviously hoped the expedition would be the answer to his prayers. Something inside of her said that joining the expedition would be a terrible mistake, but she hadn't listened to her parents as a young woman and almost missed having a family at all. If she'd married Mr. McGinness as her parents had urged, she could have stayed in Ireland as a tavern owner, but she hadn't. She knew her husband had always dreamed of owning his own land. What right did she have to take that dream from him now? Sarah would do better in a place where they were not all crowded together like chickens in a chicken coop. Agatha rose with a resigned sigh. "Very well, Mr. Colins," she said, "I will agree to this trip. Perhaps it is best for us to take our chances

now. If you'll excuse me, I must get back to my work."
With that, she left the room to resume her sewing and let
her husband show the men to the door.

Chapter 7

Even before the trip began, there was trouble. Agatha's husband hadn't been well for several days before the journey started; he was feeling weak and feverish and wasn't eating with the great appetite he usually had. Still, he refused to delay their departure. He was afraid that they'd never catch up with the other members of the expedition and that his dream of a new home for his family would end. Agatha realized that members of her family had had their share of illness in the two years they had lived in New York, but nothing serious ever came of it. Since they had already sold most of their belongings in preparation for the trip, she agreed that the delay was not worth the risk. On the day they were to depart, Agatha helped her husband pull the two-wheeled cart he had made, with all of their belongings in it, to the Hudson River dock. Their daughter, Sarah, who was now 8 years old, walked beside them.

Once on board the boat, many of the expedition members chattered excitedly about the land they would soon own, the houses they would build, and all the adventures that awaited them on this new journey. Agatha kept a close eye on her husband as Sarah played with the other children. Hearing her daughter's laughter, a sound she hadn't heard much in the last two years, Agatha thought about how much their lives had changed since they left Ireland.

As much as she had wanted children and loved her daughter, Agatha hadn't been able to spend much time with the child since they'd arrived in America. The tender words and hugs, that she once had bestowed on Sarah so liberally, had been transformed into silences born of exhaustion, and clipped commands whenever she needed to have Sarah lend her a hand or sit down to a meal. It was time, Agatha knew, to begin teaching her daughter how to sew and cook. She wanted her child to remember these lessons as a time of shared joy, not as a time of silence and drudgery. Agatha wanted it to be as special for Sarah as it had been for her as a child when her mother taught her to do delicate embroidery. She'd hoped to have time to spend with Sarah on the trip from New York to Chicago. They could talk quietly of their home in Ireland, and perhaps exchange some quiet smiles and words of hope for their new home. But the heavy workload of the last few years, and a growing concern for her husband's health on this trip, had made all attempts at tenderness feel very awkward. The love was there between mother and daughter, but the words were not. "All in due time," thought Agatha, "When we reach our destination, there will be time enough to spend with my dear Sarah."

As they traveled on the Hudson River, Agatha was able to pass off her husband's illness as sea sickness. His condition didn't get better, but he didn't get worse either, so Agatha thought he'd be well by the time they reached Buffalo. Once on the Erie Canal barge, however, Agatha noticed that her husband had become more feverish and that there was a wheezing sound coming from his chest. By the time they reached Buffalo, Agatha was a widow. Her husband had died of pneumonia.

Agatha felt sorry for her husband. He hadn't lived to see his dream of owning his own land come true. She knew that Sarah would miss her father terribly, but there was no time to console her now. With Robert Colins help, she must find a priest and make arrangements to bury her husband. She also had to decide if she and Sarah should continue the trip or turn back. If they wanted to go on, she would have to convince the Colins brothers that they wouldn't be a burden to their fellow travelers. This was no time to indulge in tears or regrets. They would have to be stoic. Sarah seemed to understand this and did not demand attention or comfort from her mother.

They found a priest in Buffalo who would administer Last Rites to her husband and allow him to be buried in the church graveyard. It comforted Agatha that he had been given a proper Christian burial.

Once the burial was over, everyone was anxious to continue the journey. Agatha knew that she and Sarah must join them at once or go back to New York. A decision had to be made. Knowing there was nothing for her to return to in New York, and believing that she and her daughter were made of sterner stuff than her husband, Agatha chose to continue the journey. She made this decision by the graveside, just as Robert Colins approached her, hat in hand, to offer his condolences.

"I'm sorry for your loss, Mrs. Wilson," he said. "Your husband was a good man. I know this trip was his idea, so I will help you arrange passage back to New York. There is no reason for you to continue now."

Agatha looked calmly at Robert and declared, "There is nothing to go back to, Mr. Colins. My husband is dead, and New York would be too expensive for us to live in with only me to work. We cannot afford to return to Ireland. Since we cannot go back, we must go forward."

Robert Colins looked alarmed. "But how can you manage such an undertaking on your own? We can help you during the trip, but once we reach our destination, you and your daughter will be on your own. Do you really believe you have the strength to build a house and cultivate the land? Surely you won't be up to that."

Agatha waited for a moment before replying, and then calmly said, "I made most of the arrangements for this trip, since my husband was already ill, and I learned about farming in Ireland. All Sarah and I need is company on the journey to our new home. Once there, we will manage very well. You need not worry about us. We will do our share of the work on this trip. We will not slow you down."

Robert frowned as he considered her words. Agatha extended her right hand towards him and, looking him in the eye, said, "Take my hand, Mr. Colins." He reached out reluctantly with his own right hand, not knowing what she intended to do next. Agatha gripped his hand firmly and said, "Is this the hand of a weak person, Mr. Wilson?" Her eyes never wavered from his face as he struggled to make up his mind about her future with the group. She could see his confusion, but resisted the urge to say anything else to him.

"Very well, Mrs. Wilson," he said, at last, "you may continue the journey with us. But I want you to find a family who will agree to let you and Sarah travel with them. We cannot risk losing time on the trail making sure you keep up with us."

Agatha allowed herself a brief smile of relief and then said, "You shall not regret this decision, Mr. Wilson."

As they traveled from Buffalo to Chicago on the Great Lakes the next day, Agatha's energy was spent finding another family to team up with. There was no time left over to question Sarah's quiet acceptance of her father's death. When they reached Chicago, they discovered that it consisted of a handful of residences, and a large trading post. As for Fort Dearborn, it was managed by a custodian; soldiers had not been billeted there for several years. Agatha bought her own supplies at the trading post, including a tent that she and daughter Sarah would sleep in at night. Their belongings were loaded into one of the wagons and the cart was left behind.

The first day out of Chicago, they covered very little ground. The men had to learn how to handle the oxen and wagons. Women and older children walked over the roughest terrain where they could keep up with the wagons and ease the burden on the animals. Everyone was sore and tired beyond imagining when they camped that first evening. They still had firewood to gather, meals to prepare, tents to put up and animals to settle for the night before any but the youngest children could sleep. Too tired to talk, the new pioneers fell asleep as soon as they'd finished their chores and were able to lie down.

By the third day, a little more progress was being made; they traveled nearly ten miles before they stopped for the night. People were beginning to learn their chores. Children ceased complaining about the rough road. Walking was getting easier. The trail they followed was not yet a well-beaten path, but they didn't encounter many true hills. The land stretched out forever in front of them with a grove of trees or a small settlement here and there to mark their progress. The prairie grass had grown just tall enough to hide groundhog holes that would twist the ankles of unwary newcomers. With the exception of a large encampment at the trading post, they'd encountered few Indians. Those they did see were observing them from a distance, and had been pronounced "friendly" by the expedition leaders.

That night, when the meal was done and everything was put away, Agatha lay down next to Sarah, who lay still with her back to her mother. Agatha was used to hard work, but she hadn't walked so much since she left Ireland. As a young woman, she would take long walks over the hills at home after her chores were done. She'd pass the time of day with the neighbors she encountered on these jaunts. How she'd loved the sweet smells of nature and the bright green color of the land! Agatha could feel the soft, cool breeze on her face. In spite of her aching body, she smiled at these memories. She thought of her mother and the evenings spent in the parlor listening with friends as her mother spoke of life in Boston. "Ah Mother," she said out loud, "how would you tell of our life here and of my husband who died without a wake to send him on or comfort us?"

Then, for the first time since the trip began, Agatha heard her daughter crying quietly. "My words must have upset her," thought Agatha. "I must take hold of my feelings or I will frighten her." She reached over to the unhappy child and stroked her hair gently. "Don't worry, Sarah," she said softly, "Your mother will always be here to take care of you. You know that." Sarah nodded her head without turning toward her mother; she stiffened her back and, after letting out a few sobs, brought herself under control. It had been a long time since any tenderness had passed between them and Agatha wanted to cry too. Instead, she swallowed hard and said in a firmer voice, "There you go, my dear. We're strong. We'll be just fine. Sleep now." The next day they got up and went about the business of preparing breakfast and packing up. Nothing more was said about the tears, but Agatha wondered how her own mother might have handled it.

On the fourth day, it began to rain. The ground was becoming slippery under foot, and this slowed their progress slightly. By the fifth day, the ground was getting very muddy, and wagon wheels were mired. A few of the men cut down some small trees from a grove and used poles shaped from their trunks to pry the wheels out of the muck. They worked slowly, the sticky clay pulling at their boots, and hindering their movements. The weather had become unseasonably cold, and rain pelted them mercilessly as they struggled with the wagons. At one point, they had to seek shelter by a grove of trees as the rain turned to large hailstones that pummeled the ground and panicked the animals.

To add to their troubles, many people had taken sick, much like Agatha's husband, and, worst of all, one baby had died. There was no settlement nearby. Nothing could be done but to bury the body by the side of the trail, and move on after a few brief prayers were said over the grave.

Although they struggled to increase the distance they were traveling each day, nothing seemed to be working in their favor. Several wagons lost wheels and the men had to work out in the cold and the rain to fix them, a chore that took a long time since they weren't used to it. As some of these men became ill, the women had to take over their chores. For her part, Agatha learned to select the dry lower branches of the trees for firewood. She already knew how to pitch her own tent.

After traveling for 10 days, Robert Colins estimated that they'd only gone 40 miles. The trail had dwindled down to little better than a footpath, leaving them to cope with waist-high prairie grass, or overhanging branches and partially exposed roots in the wooded areas. The weather had improved, but so many people were sick that Robert Colins decided to set up camp in a wooded area to wait out the illness.

Chapter 8

Shattee, a Potawatomi, quietly moved closer as the pioneers set up camp. His people had tracked the progress of the white travelers since they left Chicago; their 19 wagons sounding like rolling thunder when they first set out traveling on the hard, dry ground. But bad weather and wagon mishaps soon slowed their progress dramatically. They would make good headway one day and barely cover a mile the next.

Members of Shattee's tribe near Fort Dearborn had sent word that the travelers were planning to reach California before the snow was on the ground. Shattee had heard about California before, from stories passed on from tribe to tribe. To go there, they would have to start out in the corn planting time and would not arrive until the ground was hard and cold. Since the white people had started out on this trip, news had passed through the Indian camps about the inexperience and bad luck that had so quickly hampered their journey.

As Shattee crouched in the prairie grass, a short distance from the travelers, he could see that the white chiefs were almost overwhelmed in their efforts to get the work organized. Women were distracted by sick or cranky children, leaving their men to set up the tents. In the confusion, no one was assigned to guard the camp or scout the area. When Shattee's people set up a new camp site, they chose a place close to water and posted lookouts immediately. The women of the tribe would set up the tents, gather wood, and prepare the meals, while some of the men scouted the area for sources of food and danger. As he watched them, Shattee noted that several men and women appeared to be ill and had to be helped from the wagons into the tents. Was illness was the reason for their carelessness? Did they even know how to protect themselves?

Next, Shattee observed a short, plump woman, with hair the color of a prairie fire at night, who was setting up her own tent. She moved with assurance performing her task efficiently with the help of a young girl. They communicated with each other using a few words and simple gestures. When their task was completed, the woman proceeded to gather firewood. Shattee was impressed with this woman's self-reliance.

His eyes moved again over the group. Some semblance of order was finally being established. Men unloaded provisions from the wagons and the women gathered firewood. The white chiefs sent one of the men and some of the older children to collect water from a spring they'd passed about a quarter mile back. Shattee wondered why they hadn't set up camp closer to the spring. Had exhaustion overcome these people, forcing them to stop before they reached the river, which was a half mile away? Did they know about the river nearby?

At last, one of the settlers caught a glimpse of Shattee and hurried to tell the leaders. Then, and only then, was a guard posted. Shattee, meanwhile, had had time to observe the disorganized state of the travelers and the plenitude of their provisions. This could be a great opportunity for his tribe to gain some of the settlers' goods in exchange for information about the territory and help with hunting and fishing. As more members of the expedition became aware of his presence and began looking nervously in his direction, Shattee quietly rose and walked away. He would speak to the tribal council before any greetings were exchanged with the white people.

Chapter 9

Once the weary travelers had set up camp and eaten supper, Joseph Colins asked the head of each family to attend a meeting. Not everyone came, due to sickness or exhaustion, but Agatha was there. Mr. McGrath, who shared his family's wagon with Agatha and Sarah, was able to come only because Sarah was left to watch his children while his sick wife rested.

The Colins brothers were concerned about the poor progress that had been made so far. They also worried about using up valuable food supplies while waiting for the illness to pass in the camp. At this meeting, they asked for volunteers from the group to form a hunting party that could supply the camp with meat until this crisis was over. Only four of the men who knew how to hunt were able to volunteer. Agatha, realizing that hunting was a skill she must learn before reaching her homestead, stepped forward and said, "I have never hunted, but I am quick to learn and would gladly be a member of the hunting party."

At first, Robert Colins objected to her participation, particularly since Agatha had no previous hunting experience. He refused Agatha, saying, "Thank you for your offer, but the women must stay in camp and cook for their families. You would be of more help if you gathered berries with some of the women and children. With only four volunteers, we cannot spare anyone to teach you how to handle a gun."

But Agatha wouldn't agree to this. "I am a strong, capable woman," she said, "Did I not learn quickly to fend for my own family on this trip? No one has to take care of me. As for cooking, Sarah can manage that. She can help with Mr. McGrath's family now too. She does not need me constantly by her side."

At this point, Mr. McGrath spoke up. "I know how to hunt and will be able to join the hunting party if Sarah watches over my family. Mrs. Wilson is right. Sarah is a capable young girl who can be trusted to do what cooking my family will need. As for Mrs. Wilson learning to hunt, she can stay by me. I will teach her."

Still, the leaders were reluctant to give Agatha permission, and so the discussion continued until at last Agatha said, "And what if some of this fine hunting group takes sick too? Time will have to be taken then to train new hunters. I must learn to hunt before Sarah and I settle in California. Why not teach me now?"

Seeing Agatha's determination, and knowing her accomplishments thus far, the leaders finally acquiesced. With that, the discussion broke up and people returned to their own tents. Agatha and Mr. McGrath discussed the plans with Sarah and the McGrath family. When everyone understood that Sarah would be in charge of the children and the cooking until Mrs. McGrath got better, Agatha and Sarah went back to their own tent. Once there, Agatha spent the next few hours quietly instructing Sarah on the basic points of cooking porridge, baking biscuits and preparing coffee. When this was done, Agatha asked the critical question, "You have already learned how to build the cooking fire and you have watched me prepare our meals. Do you think you will be able to cook for the McGraths so that I can go hunting, my girl?"

Sarah knew her mother was counting on her to help. She was proud that her mother believed that she was big enough to take care of the McGraths. "Yes, Mother. I can take care of everything here for you," said

Sarah, with more confidence in her voice than she really felt.

"Good," said Agatha. "Now that it is settled, we must get some sleep." Quietly, they prepared for bed. Agatha and Sarah both fell asleep quickly; too tired to worry about what lay ahead of them.

On the first day, the expedition's hunting party did not fare well. They spent most of the day looking for likely fishing places and trying to discover what quarry was available. Since hunting was new to some of them, good ammunition was wasted shooting at rabbits. Indeed, the novices made so much noise they frightened away the deer that were in the area. Late in the afternoon, the hunting party returned to camp, tired and discouraged, with little to show for their efforts. Unbeknownst to them, some Potawatomi had been observing their efforts that day and approached the camp leaders as the hunters were explaining their difficulties to the Colins brothers.

From years of acting as guides for soldiers, map makers, and hunters, not to mention all of the trading that they did with other expeditions, many of the Potawatomi had learned to speak English. Although settlers in Chicago had assured the Colins brothers that the Potawatomi were friendly, they had neglected to mention that many of the Indians had a good command of the English language. Thus, Robert and Joseph were startled to find that communication with Shattee and his party was not difficult.

Shattee explained that his group could provide information and guides to the hunting party. From years of living in the area, the Potawatomi knew the best places to fish and to hunt. They were willing to share their expertise in return for some of the expedition's supplies. As they negotiated, Robert Colins revealed that they had set up camp temporarily due to the illness that was devastating the travelers. Shattee offered to help their hunting party learn to hunt more effectively and proposed that much of the fish they needed could be provided by the Potawatomi who often fished at night. They used torches to attract fish to the surface where they could be speared. For those expedition members who wished to do their own fishing, his people could provide fish hooks made of deer bone and spears made of wood and bone. He also noted that the expedition's hunting party would do better to save their ammunition by limiting most of their hunting to snaring smaller animals and letting the Potawatomi provide them with larger game that they killed with bow and arrow. Shattee also offered to provide the expedition with some of the Potawatomi medicine for their sick members.

It took a great deal of time to negotiate a trade between the shrewd Potawatomi and the wary expedition members. At last it was agreed that some of Shattee's people would escort the expedition's hunting party for several days showing them new and more efficient ways of bringing down the game. Amongst the game available in the area were bison, black bear, deer, and smaller animals such as rabbits and wild turkey. The Potawatomi would provide them with deer and other large game, but would also show the hunters how to use a bow and arrow. The hunting party would trade some food, cooking utensils, and clothing for information, guidance, and additional game provided by Shattee and his people. Since Robert Colins was not sure if he could trust Potawatomi medicine, it was not included in the final agreement.

Over the next few days, the expedition's hunting party worked hard to absorb the hunting and fishing methods used by the Potawatomi. Soon, they were able to recognize the tracks of their desired quarry and to come upon these animals quietly. Agatha's efforts to learn equaled that of the male members of her group. Her determination and ability to learn quickly and without complaint were admired by the Potawatomi and her own people.

Meanwhile, eight-year-old Sarah was taking care of Mrs. McGrath and her three young children. Throughout the camp, people worked hard to get their chores done while taking care of their sick family members. Sarah hauled water along with the women, who gave her advice on how to prepare some simple meals. She learned quickly how to keep the McGrath children amused while she went about her chores, so that they wouldn't disturb their sick mother.

For over a week, she continued this routine while Mrs. McGrath's condition reached a crisis and then slowly began to improve. Sarah never said the work was too much for her. How could she when her mother worked so hard? But one evening when she returned to her own tent, Sarah felt too tired and ill to eat. She went directly to bed and fell into a restless sleep. Agatha assumed her daughter was eating with the McGrath's, so she didn't insist that Sarah eat with her. Late that night, the child began to shiver with the cold.

Early the next morning, as Sarah slept, the leaders went around the camp and asked the healthy men, and some women who didn't have young children to care for, to meet them at their tent. The news wasn't good. Up to this point, although many people were ill, only a few had died. They were buried by their own family members and every able-bodied person in the camp would join in a prayer by the grave of the person who had died. Now, however, more than half of the pioneers were sick and four people had died in the night. In some wagons, there was no one left healthy enough to prepare food or care for the sick. Every healthy adult was now required to perform all of the chores for the group. This meant that meals would now be prepared at one main campfire instead of wagon by wagon. Several of the women volunteered to prepare breakfast and left to get organized. Others agreed to help by caring for the sick in families overwhelmed by this illness. Since Agatha was mastering the skills of hunting and fishing, she was asked to continue with the men in that group. Two men volunteered to dig the graves for the four who had died, but it was agreed that there would not be time for a service until dusk.

Agatha began thinking of the baby they had buried two weeks before on the side of the road and of the people they would bury tonight. There was no priest among the members of the wagon train to say the right words over the graves. A makeshift wooden cross would mark the graves for a short time, but soon even this acknowledgment of their loved ones would disappear. Agatha could not imagine leaving a family member behind like that. She thanked the Lord again that her husband had received better than this.

Agatha was still lost in thought when Mr. McGrath approached. She hadn't noticed him, so she was startled when he said, in a gruff voice, "Mrs. Wilson, I want to thank you for letting Sarah take care of my family this past week."

Agatha looked up, startled from her thoughts. "How is the Missus now?" she asked.

"She is feeling much better, and the kids are healthy too, thanks to Sarah's good care," he replied with a smile. "I shall bring my family their breakfast as soon as the women have it ready. Please let Sarah sleep late with our thanks."

Agatha smiled back and nodded; inside she beamed with pride. Imagine, her Sarah, just eight years old, was able to take care of a family so well and without complaint. She knew now she could rely on Sarah to help her with the land when they reached their homestead in California.

Returning to her tent to get ready for the day's hunting, Agatha noticed that Sarah was restless and moaning in her sleep. She decided to get some breakfast herself before waking her daughter with the good news about the McGrath family. Agatha ate fried fish, berries and a dry biscuit, which she washed down with strong coffee, before returning to the tent. The sun had been shining on the tent for a little while and it was getting stuffy. This time, Agatha knelt down beside Sarah and gently shook her daughter's shoulder. "Sarah. Sarah. Time to get up, my girl, and have some breakfast."
Sarah mumbled something but did not wake up. Agatha noticed that her daughter's hair was matted and that she her brow was sweaty. She smoothed Sarah's hair back with her hand. Sarah felt a little warm. "Sarah," Agatha said firmly, "'Tis time. Get up now. It is too hot here for you to stay asleep. You must get up and eat your breakfast with the others."
Sarah opened her eyes slightly. Squinting at her mother she mumbled something about wanting to sleep more. "No, Sarah," said Agatha. "I must leave now to go hunting. You do not have to fix anyone's meals today but the McGrath family will still need your help. I hear things are much better for them now. You've done a good job so far. Now please get up. Do not disappoint me."
Sarah, forcing herself awake as her mother stood up to leave, managed to get into a sitting position and rubbed her eyes. "Are you feeling all right?" Agatha asked. Sarah's head was pounding, but she did not want to trouble her mother.

"I'm fine, Mother," Sarah replied.

Agatha sighed with relief. For a moment there, she had feared her Sarah would get sick like the others. But she was fine after all. She was strong like her mother. "Hurry then," said Agatha. "Everyone is eating together now. Better go get something to eat before it is all gone." With that, Agatha left.

Sarah slowly struggled to her feet, pulled her nightgown off and, fumbling, tried to put on her brown dress quickly as she shivered. She was cold to the bone. "How can I be cold now? I was hot not one minute ago," thought Sarah, becoming a little frightened.

She pulled a shawl over her shoulders and left the tent. The sunlight made her head hurt more. She squinted her eyes and headed to the campfire where the women were dishing out food. As she got closer, the smell of the food made her stomach churn. Sarah decided that breakfast was not such a good idea after all. "It would be best just to start taking care of Mrs. McGrath and the children," she thought.

She turned quickly towards their wagon and was hit with a sudden dizzy spell. She paused, rocking in place until the dizziness passed. By now fresh beads of sweat were running down her face. "I will be all right," she reassured herself. "Mother said we are both strong. She is well. I will be well too." Taking a deep breath she moved on to the wagon and the waiting children.

Helen McGrath was sitting up talking to her young children when Sarah arrived. They had already eaten breakfast and Mrs. McGrath was beginning to feel much healthier. Looking at Sarah, she recognized the early signs of the illness as she'd experienced them. "You look rather peaked, Sarah," said Mrs. McGrath. "Are you feeling well?"

"I'm fine, thank you," said Sarah, automatically. It was the polite thing to say, but it wasn't true. Still, Sarah remembered her mother saying once that, when people asked how you were, they really didn't want to know.

"You don't look too well, Sarah. Have you had your breakfast yet?" asked Mrs. McGrath, her concern growing as she realized that Sarah was leaning on the wagon for support.

"I'm not really hungry," said Sarah. "Do you want me to dress the children now?" Sarah's words might have sounded more convincing had her throat not gone quite dry. The words she spoke came out in a croak. "I just need a drink of water," said Sarah, trying to cover for this weakness.

Mrs. McGrath nodded and watched as Sarah reached for the dipper sitting by a large pail of water. Sarah scooped some water up out of the pail and began to drink. The water felt so cool in her mouth. It eased the parched feeling in her throat. She hadn't realized how thirsty she was. Sarah took another dipper full of water and drank it in several long gulps. As she replaced the dipper, her stomach rebelled and she was violently ill by the side of the wagon.

Mrs. McGrath got up as quickly as she could, wet a piece of cloth with water from the dipper and took it over to Sarah. By now, Sarah was trembling all over, her knees were weak and she needed to lean hard against the wagon in order not to fall. Mrs. McGrath put her arm around Sarah's shoulder to support the child and gently wiped Sarah's face with the cool damp cloth.

Late that afternoon when Agatha returned from hunting, she discovered that Mrs. McGrath was now tending Sarah. Mrs. McGrath had summoned one of the other women in the camp to get Sarah's nightgown from

101

Agatha's tent. It had taken both women to change Sarah from her restrictive brown dress into the looser, cooler nightgown. But to Sarah now, nothing was cool. She needed water, but couldn't keep it down. A battle was raging in her throat that rendered her unable to speak above a whisper.

Agatha knelt in the wagon beside her daughter, who was quite pale and sleeping fitfully. "How could I have missed the signs of this illness in Sarah? Did it just start today, or was she sick last night? Will she get better?" These thoughts raced through Agatha's mind as she looked down upon her daughter.

Several more people had died today, and the leaders were talking about a mass grave because they couldn't spare the men to dig more. Moreover, the grave diggers had grown too tired to dig very deeply, so they had to fetch rocks from the river to place over each new mound of earth. The rocks were necessary to keep animals away. "Surely God, Sarah will be spared!" thought Agatha, desperate not to lose the last of her family.

She bent closer to her sleeping daughter and gently smoothed the hair back from Sarah's hot face. As she did this, Agatha thought of Sarah's behavior over the last few days. "How long has Sarah been ill?" she wondered feeling guilty. "Could I have done anything to stop this if I'd seen it coming?"

Agatha frowned as she thought how busy she had been learning to fish and hunt like the men, believing the child didn't need her help. She'd been preparing for the day she and Sarah would be on their own, but she had expected too much of her young daughter. Anger at her own shortsightedness grew, deepening the frown on her face.

Sarah opened her eyes as a spasm of pain turned her stomach into a knot. Seeing her Mother, she tried to sit up. She could see by Agatha's frown how disappointed she must be. "I'm sorry, Mother," Sarah whispered.

"Nonsense, my girl!" Agatha said in a husky voice, "We shall go back to our own tent now. You will be better in no time."

Sarah hated to be moved. Every part of her body hurt, but she was careful not to complain. Mr. McGrath, having returned from hunting with Agatha, helped get the sick little girl back to her own tent. Agatha fetched a fresh pail of spring water and began the process of cooling Sarah's brow and offering her sips of water. For the next 3 days, she tended to her daughter day and night. Agatha tried to get her now frail child to take some refreshment. Water, tea and thin porridge were coaxed into Sarah, but nothing would stay down.

Meanwhile, the epidemic continued to spread throughout the camp. The death toll mounted almost daily, adding more bodies to the mass grave. Few were spared the illness, but some were luckier than most and were able to function in spite of their symptoms. Others, particularly the very old and very young, did not survive.

In a little less than 2 weeks, 15 people died. Sarah was among the last to get sick and Agatha prayed fervently for her quick recovery.

Sarah had tried so hard to get better, to show her mother she was strong after all. But the fever wouldn't let up. Gradually, her eyes became dull and lifeless. On the last day, she slipped into unconsciousness. Now and again she would cry out for her mother. Agatha stayed close by, reassuring her daughter that she was not alone, but the child couldn't hear her. Then Sarah's breathing developed a rattle. Agatha watched in horror on that final afternoon as her daughter's breathing became more labored, and then stopped.

Agatha, totally exhausted from worry and lack of sleep, could not at first comprehend the silence in the tent. She stared down at her child, so thin and pale. Sarah's lips were slightly parted, but no breath came from them. Agatha bent down and listened, her ear close to Sarah's mouth, but still no sound came. She couldn't believe this was happening. Not again. She couldn't lose her last child. Something must be done! Agatha ran from the tent to the McGrath's wagon, crying, "Help! My poor Sarah! Help me!"

Mr. McGrath raced to the tent with Agatha close behind. He went inside and examined Sarah quickly. There was nothing to be done. He felt so sad for this little girl who had played such an important role in saving his own family. He turned to leave the tent when he realized that Agatha had come back into it. "I am so sorry, Mrs. Wilson. There is nothing to be done. Sarah is gone."

Agatha stared at Mr. McGrath. "No!" she said in disbelief. She knelt down beside her daughter's still body. "Sarah?" she cried. "Sarah, can you hear me? Wake up!" Agatha strained her ears, but no sound came from Sarah's tiny body. Mr. McGrath did not know what to do to help Agatha. She'd always been so matter of fact and self sufficient. He reached down and gently rested a hand on her shoulder to try to comfort her. Agatha moved her shoulder violently to escape the comfort he offered. "No!" she said angrily. "She cannot be dead." "Sarah, wake up for Mother," Agatha pleaded as she gathered her daughter up in her arms. But Sarah's head fell back from Agatha's bosom and the final breath of air left in Sarah's body escaped in a long sigh.

Gently, Agatha laid her daughter's body back down as the full impact of Sarah's death hit her. She had not brought her precious daughter from Ireland for this! To die in the wilderness. No priest here to free her soul. No grandmother there to help prepare a wake. Agatha felt like she couldn't breathe. She reached up to the collar of her dress and began to tear at it, trying to force it open with her bare hands. The sound of ripping cloth mixed with a sound that started as a low moan of denial and seemed to come from the depths of Agatha's being. It grew to a wail as she continued to tear at her clothing.

Mr. McGrath backed out of the tent in panic and ran for help. He was no match for her grief. The sound of Agatha's despair was so overwhelming that it stopped people in their tracks. It made the blood run cold in all who heard it. Children stopped playing and ran in terror to find their mothers. The birds stopped singing and listened as this strange sound grew ever louder and more frightening. It built to an eerie, high-pitched shriek of despair that seemed to last forever. Like the shriek of a banshee, surely it could be heard in all of Ireland, too.

Gradually, the sound died down, to be followed by Agatha's sobbing and crying. People in the camp began to go about their chores again, slowly, quietly, not wanting to provoke another such outburst. Nobody wanted to approach Agatha in this state. Mr. McGrath and the other men agreed to wait until her crying had ceased before approaching her tent.

It was late in the evening when Agatha finally fell into an exhausted sleep. The men waited until the first light of morning to creep into her tent and remove the child's body. Sarah would be buried quickly. She was the last to die.

It was time to move on. Better for everyone to leave this place immediately, the men decided. They would pack everything up before waking Agatha, then the women could help her dress and pack her things.

When everything was packed and ready to go, there would be time for one last prayer over the grave before they left this horror behind. The leaders had decided that they could not make it to California now, but they wanted to get as far west as possible before stopping for the winter. They'd decide then whether to disband or move on the following spring.

Although there were no new or serious cases of the sickness now, some of the people were still weak and would not be able to walk much for a while. Robert ordered the travelers to lighten the load in their wagons as much as possible, to let the recuperating members of the party ride in more comfort. It was hard for people to give up the precious items they'd brought with them, but they knew it was necessary. They took their clothes and linens out of cedar chests and left these heavy containers by the side of the road. Some people had brought family pictures, furniture, or china that they now realized took up too much room. Where possible, dry goods that had been stored in barrels were transferred to pillow cases and the barrels were discarded. These changes allowed the travelers to redistribute the load in their wagons to make room for ailing group members. Robert hoped these changes would also ease the burden on the oxen enough so they could make up some of the time lost on this trip.

When everyone else was packed, the women went cautiously into Agatha's tent to help her. Agatha was calm as she woke up. She cooperated with the women as they got her into fresh clothing and brushed her hair. Much of what had happened the previous day had been mercifully forgotten by Agatha, but she knew now that Sarah was dead. She quietly packed up her belongings and left the tent to join the others in prayer. But as she approached the grave site, she realized, to her horror, that Sarah was in a large grave shared by the others who had died. This would not do! Sarah could not have a priest, but at least she could have a grave of her own. Agatha knew what she must do. She approached the grave diggers and asked where, specifically, her daughter had been put so that she could stand close by. Nervously, the men pointed to the farthest end of the grave. Agatha nodded and went to that spot. She stood in prayer with the others. Afterwards, they all sang a hymn and then the group broke up as people went to their wagons to make final preparations.

Agatha approached Mr. McGrath who was about to load her belongings into his wagon. "I want to thank you, Mr. McGrath, for all the help you have given to Sarah and me on this journey. I will remember your kindness always," said Agatha in a calm voice. "But please do not pack my things. I will be staying here." Mr. McGrath thought that Agatha didn't understand.

"We are ready to leave now, Mrs. Wilson," he said. "We can go as soon as I take down your tent and put your belongings in my wagon. It will be better for all of us to get away from this place and its sad memories."

"It is not better for me," Agatha said firmly. "I have nothing to go to. My family is gone now. I must stay by Sarah." Mr. McGrath hurried away to inform the Colins brothers of Agatha's intentions. They conferred for a few moments and then Robert Colins approached Agatha, with his brother Joseph and Mr. McGrath following close behind him.

"Is something wrong, Mrs. Wilson?" Robert asked. "I hear you are not ready to leave yet. Do you need to spend a few more hours here? Should we say another prayer for Sarah?"

"I am fine, Mr. Colins," said Agatha. "You need not wait any longer; so much time has been lost already. Please go, with my blessings and prayers for everyone."

"But you cannot mean to stay here on your own! There are no nearby settlements to move to. Come with us," urged Robert. "We can use your help with the hunting and fishing as we travel and you need people to help you too."

"I need no one now," Agatha said sadly. "My family is gone. I have only Sarah's memory for comfort. I want to be near her. As for my hunting and fishing skills, that will serve me well right here. I know the Indians now and will trade with them while I have goods to trade. Soon someone will settle here and I can get a priest to come and say a few words over Sarah."

Joseph and Mr. McGrath joined in with Robert in a continued effort to change her mind, but hours passed and still Agatha would not be persuaded to leave. Her hysteria of the previous day had been replaced by grim determination. Something in Agatha's attitude told the men that she could not be budged on this. They were afraid to try to force her since she might lose control again. As time went on, other members of the expedition came over to find out what was happening, and joined in trying to persuade Agatha to leave with them. Finally, Mrs. McGrath spoke quietly with her husband, who then told Agatha that she would be more than welcome to become part of his family.

"Thank you again for trying to help me, Mr. McGrath," she said, "but I must not leave my daughter. She deserves to be remembered. If I leave now, no one will know she ever existed; no priest will bless her grave. If you were in my shoes, what would you do?" Agatha looked steadily at Mr. McGrath, waiting for him to understand her position and lend his support.

Mr. McGrath had great respect for Agatha. He felt sure that she could take care of herself in almost any situation. If she needed help, he knew the Indians were close at hand. Mr. McGrath took Robert and Joseph aside and convinced them to give in to her. They didn't want to leave her, but they couldn't stay here any longer; too much time had already been lost. Reluctantly, they agreed to leave her behind with her share of the provisions.

"Her supplies will surely outlast her willingness to stay by the grave," said Robert, at last. "It troubles me to leave her here, but the Indians have been helpful to us all and will certainly continue to trade with her." Robert wondered to himself if the Indian medicine could have helped prevent so many deaths. It was too late to do anything about that, but perhaps he could arrange for the Potawatomi to help Mrs. Wilson get back to Chicago, once she finally gave up on the idea of waiting for a priest.

After further discussion, the men decided to leave her a musket and ammunition, as well as her share of the food. She already had her own tent, ax, shovel, and water pail. In addition, Agatha would have the goods that the others were leaving behind, to use or trade.

"We will leave you then, Mrs. Wilson," said Mr. McGrath sadly. "You and Sarah will always be in our prayers." With that said, the leaders went around the camp telling everyone to be ready to leave immediately. Quietly, Agatha said her good-byes to the McGraths and a few other families she had befriended. As the wagon train moved off into the distance, Agatha took the shovel and began digging a new grave for Sarah, near her tent, and away from the mass grave.

By evening of the following day, she had located Sarah's body and, wrapping the child in her best shawl, Agatha tenderly laid Sarah in her new resting place. She covered the grave with earth, and placed some rocks from the mass grave on top of Sarah's to keep the animals away. Then, she gathered wildflowers to place on top of the stones, and fashioned a cross with twigs and vines to mark the grave. Finally, she scratched Sarah's name at the foot of the grave with the sharp edge of a twig. Now Sarah's body lay safe near Agatha and no one would disturb it again. Agatha would see to that.

Chapter 10

Shattee and his hunting party encountered the Colins' expedition shortly after the pioneers had taken their leave of Agatha and the mass grave. The hunters waited until Robert Colins had brought his group to a halt, and then Shattee stepped forward to say good-bye, and possibly to do some final trading. Several of the men, including Mr. McGrath, left their wagons to join Robert. Shattee could see by the worried looks on the white men's faces that something was troubling them. The sun was shining in the sky and the travelers were no longer getting sick, so Shattee was puzzled by their unhappiness. He paused, looked up into the sky and then slowly scanned the wagons before returning his gaze to Robert. "It is a good day to leave," said Shattee and then he waited for someone to tell him what was wrong.

"It is a good day," replied Robert, nodding, but with a face that still reflected his concerns. "We have a serious problem and need your help. We are concerned about Mrs. Wilson. You know her; she was a member of our hunting party. Her daughter just died and Mrs. Wilson has refused to leave the grave. She cannot stay long by the graveside, but we could not make her come with us. She may not change her mind for weeks, so we had to leave her behind. We are very worried about her safety."

Shattee was surprised to hear that Mrs. Wilson would not continue the trip. He knew what a strong woman she was, after watching her learn to hunt and fish, and seeing how she behaved in the camp. He was not surprised that the men could not make her go against her will, but he thought she would know the danger of staying alone. "We know Mrs. Wilson," said Shattee and waited for more information.

"We believe that Mrs. Wilson will want to return to Chicago once she is over the shock of her daughter's death. But until she is ready, we would like your people to keep an eye on her. Once she knows she cannot stay here alone, someone must help her get to Fort Dearborn in Chicago, where she can seek shelter until she knows where she wants to settle," Robert paused and then, looking around at the men who had assembled with him, he continued. "We would be willing to trade with you; some of our supplies in exchange for you watching out for her and escorting her back to the fort when she is ready."

Shattee listened with interest to Robert's proposal. He would have kept an eye on Mrs. Wilson without any trading because she was a brave woman who would need some help to survive. His people could always use some extra supplies, though. Since the travelers were interested in making this into a trading opportunity, Shattee decided to negotiate with them for bread and coffee. They would eat the bread, and could use the coffee for trading with other pioneers. He also knew that, without a trade, the white men would not be sure that his people would look out for her. Unlike Robert, Shattee did not believe the woman would be easily discouraged; and so the negotiations began.

Since his people could trade one fish for a thick slice of the pioneers' bread, they finally agreed to trade three loaves of bread in return for Shattee and his men looking out for the woman. Shattee then watched as Mr. McGrath and Joseph went around the camp collecting coffee from each family. At last, the men came back to

Shattee and Robert with a small sack of green coffee beans. The bread was to be used immediately, but the travelers stipulated that the coffee was not to be used until Mrs. Wilson had been safely accompanied back to Chicago. Shattee spoke with the other members of his hunting party and then returned to Robert saying, "We will trade."

Once the agreement was reached, Mr. McGrath stepped forward and said, "Mrs. Wilson is a proud woman. She must not know that we have asked you to watch out for her." Shattee agreed not to tell the woman about the trade. It was his intention to help her discreetly, as long as her strength and dignity allowed. He and his fellow hunters looked forward to sharing the bread with their people; but they believed that, since Mrs. Wilson was a fearless and hardworking woman who would not be turned back easily, it would be a long time before they could use the coffee.

Since responsibility for Agatha's well-being had been passed from the Colins' expedition to the Indians, Shattee and the other hunters decided to confer a new name upon her. It was customary for a member of his tribe to have several names over the course of a lifetime. The name given at birth would be changed if certain unique characteristics of the child suggested a new one. Shattee himself had had one other name. Thus Agatha Wilson unknowingly became Left Alone Woman.

Chapter 11

Agatha stood in the doorway of her hut and looked out at the sunrise. The golden glow filtered through the oak and hickory trees, raising her spirits. "It will be a fine day," she thought. "Time to prepare the garden for the growing season." She was glad the cold weather was finally over. This past winter had been very hard on her. The cold had seemed to go straight through her bones, making each movement slow and painful, as though her body were freezing into place. Agatha's hair, which had once been deep red in color, was now quite gray. Even her back, which she had always held so straight, was bending under the weight of time and cold weather and isolation. But now the warmer weather was coming and she could feel the pain and stiffness leaving her body. The earth was becoming soft enough to dig into. At last, she could begin her garden and fix up Sarah's grave.

It was the spring of 1831. Nearly a year had passed since Agatha persuaded the members of the California expedition to go on without her. They had left her with her share of food and supplies, including tobacco for trading and a musket and powder for hunting deer and for self-defense. She also had a shovel and hoe for gardening, as well as the remaining berries they'd gathered, and some of the fish they'd caught during their forced encampment. They had not been able to spare any livestock for her, however. She would have rely on heavy boots and shanks' mare when hunting, fetching water, or scouting the area for new settlers. Agatha had always enjoyed her long walks in Ireland, in all kinds of weather. But walking on the prairie in winter had been a very different matter. She was glad now she had kept her dead husband's clothing. His heavy pants had allowed her to move through the deep snow that drifted across the land in winter. Her dresses would have made such travel an impossibility.

When she wasn't hunting, fishing, or gardening, she spent her time tending to her daughter's grave, gathering wild flowers for it in the good weather, and talking for hours to Sarah's spirit. Agatha needed to constantly replenish her food stores, though she was careful with her supplies, and particularly avoided wasting gun powder. Instead, she'd chosen to snare small animals using fishing line. She caught fish, or traded for fish and larger game with the Potawatomi.

Agatha usually traded bread for fish, but on one occasion in early autumn she had offered tobacco instead, without realizing how sacred tobacco was in the Indian ceremonies. The Indians had approached her soon after and offered to provide her with a warm hut in exchange for a large pouch of tobacco. She accepted their offer, since the tent she was staying in offered little protection from dampness during the long rainy days of autumn. The Indians had left and returned a short time later with some of their women who built Agatha a house with a bed that was up off the damp ground.

Several small children accompanied the women and played nearby as the women constructed the wigwam for her. She'd enjoyed watching as the children played with each other. She noticed that their play involved imitating the work the women were doing. The women had gathered and bent the poles that would form the backbone of the wigwam. The children, in their turn, gathered twigs and attempted to form the same dome shape from them. It had been a pleasure for Agatha to watch healthy, happy young children at play again.

The wigwam that was to be Agatha's home was made of wood and rawhide with bark shingles. There was a hole in the center of the roof to allow smoke to escape and a fire pit in the floor, enabling her to cook indoors. A simple wooden cot was constructed and placed against the wall of the hut. Agatha could use the bedding she had been saving to use in her new home in California. She saw that the wigwam would allow her to be warm and dry at night, and that she could cook indoors when it was too cold or wet to do so comfortably outside.

Thinking back on that day again, Agatha was grateful for the wigwam the women had built for her. She knew now that she could not have survived the winter in her tent. At first she used the tent to store her supplies, but the ravages of winter and the damage done by hungry animals had rendered it useless even for storage. She rolled up the remnants of the tent and stored it, along with her supplies, in the hut. She was learning the Potawatomi practice of saving materials for some future purpose. The tent was a tent no longer, but its remains might come in useful someday.

On this beautiful spring morning, Agatha went out with her shovel and began to turn the soil for the garden. It was a slow process, but she didn't mind. What else was there for her to do? Some Indians came by to tell her that several white families were settling within a day's walk from her. Agatha's eyes lit up as they had not done in years. A lilt came back into her voice as she asked if there was a priest among the new settlers. When she heard that no priest had been seen, the light left Agatha's eyes once again. "They are no use to me then," was all she said. Bending over her shovel,

Agatha resumed her work.   The Indians left without another word.

Late in the day, Agatha went over to Sarah's grave. The stones that had been placed on top of it the previous year were no longer needed to keep the animals away.   Agatha was careful not to waste any of her resources, so she'd taken the stones from Sarah's grave and used them to build up the sides of her fire pit. The ground on top of Sarah's grave was smooth, and she was able to draw Sarah's name across the top, by the cross. Now, she knelt down and, smoothing the soil with her hands as if it were a child's blanket, she whispered, "I'm sorry, Sarah, there is no priest here yet to say God's words over you. We must wait a while longer." Agatha sat lost in thought about how things might have been for her and Sarah if only they hadn't left Ireland.   As darkness fell and the air grew cooler, Agatha roused herself and returned to the hut to light the fire and prepare her evening meal.

That summer more settlers moved into the area. Agatha acquired neighbors when Joseph Naper, his brother and some friends, settled nearby with their families.   She heard the first, distant sounds of construction when Joseph Naper built his log home, a trading post, and a grist mill. He'd even begun building a saw mill. All of this was taking place about one half mile southeast of her hut, but several groves of trees sheltered her hut from sight and muffled the noise of the settlers' efforts.

Agatha had changed a great deal in the year she had been on her own. She now lacked the ambition and excitement that must feed the lives of pioneers. For the time being at least, Agatha chose not to reveal herself to the newcomers.   She decided instead to reserve her energy for the day-to-day maintenance of her food supply, her lifeline. She could not afford the luxury of time off to meet these people. At the very least, she would have to answer their inevitable questions, to satisfy their curiosity or justify her decision to live as she did. At worst, they might be alarmed to discover a white woman living alone and try to take her away from Sarah's grave.

Agatha avoided entering the Potawatomi encampment. As a child, she'd always enjoyed listening to the conversations that went on between her parents and their guests, but she seldom had much to contribute herself. Having been on her own for some time now, she was even less inclined to make polite conversation. When Shattee of some of the others from his camp came to see her, there was always some business to discuss: trade, or information about the number of settlers coming into the area. She never wanted to be put in the position of visitor, since that might entail a great deal of talking on her part. No. She preferred to spend what little idle time she had sitting by Sarah's grave, watching the fireflies flicker in the peaceful evening.

It was not difficult for Agatha to maintain her privacy, since the newcomers, who were concentrating on building up their community, had little time to wander far from their work. Whereas their days bustled with activity and noise, Agatha's days were quiet and solitary. She snared small animals or fished, and tended to her garden on a daily basis. Depending upon the Indians for news of the settlers, Agatha was glad to hear that their homes were being built east of the saw mill, away from her hut. Each day, she ate breakfast by Sarah's grave as the sun came up. Then, after cleaning up and checking on the state of her garden, she would tend to her traps or fish in the DuPage River. Her hunting and fishing efforts took her north, away from the noise of the settlers, to quiet areas where she would have more success with her quarry. Late in the day, she would again work on her garden before eating dinner by Sarah's grave and preparing to turn in for the night.

Since Agatha had begun wearing her late husband's clothing the previous winter, she'd discovered she liked the physical freedom the garments gave her. His hat offered her head protection from the weather without hindering her peripheral vision. She also liked to move quickly, unfettered by the long dresses that society dictated for women. When the weather improved, Agatha decided to continue wearing men's clothing. There was no one around to criticize her for this choice: her family was gone; the Indians didn't seem to notice; and the settlers didn't even know of her existence.

In the spring, when the ground was soft and muddy, her feet would sometimes sink deep into the mire; she was glad then of her husband's boots. But sometimes in her haste, she would stumble into a boggy area. The muck would rise up past her boot tops and ooze in, filling them like soft, cold cement that anchored her feet as she struggled to free herself. It could take hours to rescue her boots and pull herself out of the bog to the firmer soil that was close by. After a few such episodes, Agatha learned to walk more slowly, with her eyes closely examining the ground ahead.

As Agatha's life became more slow-moving and peaceful, she wondered how she had ever tolerated the cacophony of life in New York. She was glad that great walls of trees separated her from the newcomers and deadened the sound of their activity. The Indians kept Agatha informed about events in the settlement. She learned that the number of settlers was increasing. By the end of the summer, Joseph Naper and a partner had established a trading post, where they traded with settlers and Indians alike, but still there was no church being built and no minister or priest in the area. Once a week, the settlement grew quiet. Shattee had explained that, at those times, the settlers were gathered in one home to pray and sing. They were taking turns holding their own Sunday services without a clergyman.

On a few occasions, people passing through the area came across Agatha's hut with the small garden, Sarah's grave, and the discards from her fellow pioneers surrounding it. The newcomers never saw Agatha near the hut. She'd be warned of their approach by the noise they made, and would conceal herself in a grove of trees until they'd safely passed by. Her hut, having been built by the Indians, was actually a wigwam, and people who saw it assumed that an Indian was camping there. They were not surprised to see the small grave, and the items left by earlier travelers, since these were familiar sights along the pioneer trail. Agatha was amazed at how little these strangers understood what was in front of them. None of them appeared to find it strange that there was only one wigwam in sight. They didn't even notice that the discards were weather-worn, while the grave was freshly tended.

Now and again, Agatha was spotted by the river, but she was always seen as a distant figure in men's clothing. Since her appearance aroused no curiosity, she realized that she must have been mistaken for one of the men from the settlement, or a stranger passing through the area. To her relief, the settlers remained unaware that a white woman lived on her own nearby, and the Indians never spoke to them of Left Alone Woman.

By the following winter, the settlers had constructed a school for their children. With so much work to be done in the settlement, even toddlers were sent to school; this allowed their parents to concentrate on making the area more hospitable. They had expected to be more self sufficient by harvest time, and were concerned that their remaining supplies might not last until spring.

Agatha heard that this was a rough time for the settlers, but their plight meant little to her. She struggled through a long, cold winter that Shattee would later describe as the worst in his memory. This was her second year alone, and she knew that the bitter weather was taking its toll on her. The icy wind and low temperatures made her body so stiff that she had trouble getting her work done. Some part of her seemed to be aching all of the time, but she forced herself to ignore the pain and get on with the business of surviving until a priest could be found. She had chores to do each day that could not be ignored if she was to continue living on her own. Still, Agatha found that she had to stop more frequently to catch her breath as she worked. In her heart, she remained committed to waiting by Sarah until her grave could be properly blessed, but her body was slowly betraying her.

When the winter came to an end, Agatha thanked God that she'd survived. She was especially grateful when Shattee told her that some of the men from the settlement had had to travel a great distance during the winter to purchase emergency provisions.

Spring of 1832 brought the sounds of renewed activity to Agatha's ears, as the settlers completed construction of the saw mill, and began preparing their land for crops. The air seemed filled with hope. She could feel her own strength and resolve returning; although she wasn't as strong as the year before.

One day, during planting season, Shattee and another Potawatomi named Bear Hunter approached

Agatha as she tended her garden. They had come to warn her that a Sauk named Black Hawk was preparing to do battle with the white settlers. Shattee explained that Black Hawk led a group of Indians who were bitter over the loss of their land to white squatters; they wanted war and enlisted the aid of other tribes. The chiefs of the Potawatomi refused to support the war, and decided to send some of their own men out to warn the settlers.

Shattee urged Agatha to leave and seek shelter at Fort Dearborn, but she refused. "Why should I leave my home?" she asked indignantly. "I have cheated no one. I spend my days quietly, tending to my chores and Sarah's grave. I will not leave her behind and run away."

Gesturing in the direction of the settlement, which to Agatha's dismay was growing quite large, she added, "Go and warn the people in the settlement. They may want to seek shelter at the fort. But do not tell them I am here; that would just make trouble for me. I can take care of myself. I have a gun should I need it; but I will not move!"

To Agatha's relief, Shattee wasted no more time arguing with her. He nodded once and went on his way to warn others.

Chapter 12

Shattee was not surprised by Left Alone Woman's answer. He rode off to warn the other settlers in the surrounding area. Left Alone Woman was well known to his people. Because of her obsessive devotion to her daughter's grave, she was considered to be "touched by the moon." His people would not harm someone like that. She would be safe, but she was entitled to choose between staying and fleeing.

Although the Potawatomi chiefs had refused to join Black Hawk, they'd given permission for individual warriors to join in the war if they wanted to. This was in keeping with the tradition of the Potawatomi. They were a fierce tribe who had defeated settlers, soldiers, and other tribes in the past. The people listened to the chiefs, but were not absolutely bound to follow them. In battle, they were known for striking their enemy suddenly and leaving as soon as the element of surprise had vanished. Other tribes were more likely to stay in the battle, once it was joined, until one side or the other had clearly been victorious. The Potawatomi method conserved the warriors, and inspired terror in their enemies.

As more and more soldiers and settlers moved into the area, however, it became clear to Shattee's people that they could not ultimately defeat the white men. No matter how many soldiers they killed, more came to take their place. The chiefs decided that they would be better off befriending the settlers. They believed that this would enable them to stay on the land while other tribes were being driven from it.

Shattee's own people moved to different camp sites depending on the season. Some locations were better for hunting, while others would provide richer soil for planting, and there were particular groves of trees they sought for the sap to make their sugar. They were accustomed to returning to the same camp sites at will, but recently they were discovering that settlers were moving into these areas and were not willing to share the land. Because of this, some of the Potawatomi were prepared to join in the battle, even though their chiefs refused to support Black Hawk.

Although he chose not to join Black Hawk, Shattee understood the warrior's anger. Each year, settlers would squat on land his people had cultivated, and then use the soldiers to evict the tribes from it. In an effort to get away from the settlers and end these land disputes, Black Hawk's people had moved west of the Mississippi River at the end of the last gathering season. But when planting time came again, they knew they could not grow all the food that was needed at the new site. Cultivating enough new land to support a village took more than one growing season. To keep from starving, some of Black Hawk's people returned to plant and tend their crops on the old site, as they always had. But their land had already been claimed by white settlers, and when they tried to take it back, the soldiers stopped them. Even an appeal to the Great White Father in Washington was refused.

Black Hawk had asked the chiefs of the Potawatomi to join forces with him and drive the settlers off the land. Although the chiefs understood his reasons, and some had no love for the white men, they believed that they could not ultimately defeat the soldiers and settlers. Instead, they chose messengers to warn the settlers of the coming war, and escort them to safety if necessary. This was a risky task for Shattee and the other messengers, since Black Hawk's supporters would have killed them if they caught them aiding the settlers.

Shattee traveled about the countryside, to the scattered settlements and isolated cabins, to urge the settlers to seek shelter at the nearest fort. Not all of them would listen, however, and many of those paid with their lives. Some who heeded the Potawatomi warning wanted to be escorted to safety. Shattee was willing to accompany settlers to safety if they asked, but he did not waste any time on those who foolishly chose to stay behind. Left Alone Woman was the exception.

She reminded him of the women of his tribe who were brave enough to become warriors. They did not ask for extra consideration, and neither did Left Alone Woman. She was wise enough to appreciate the danger, but she simply would not abandon her daughter's grave. In any case, unlike the warrior women in his tribe, Left Alone Woman lived alone. Planting season was beginning and the woman would have to plant and tend her garden. Shattee admired her courage and, above all, remembering his promise to the expedition leaders, he felt responsible for her safety. He would watch over her under the guise of friendly visits wherein he could give her news of the war and see if she needed anything.

It took time to warn everyone. By now there were close to 200 people in the nearby Naper Settlement alone. The women and children were evacuated to Fort Dearborn, which was the closest fort. Since the trails had become easier to follow in the two years it had taken to begin the Naper Settlement, they were able to cover the same forty mile distance in two days that the Colins expedition had covered in ten. They were also blessed with better weather for their flight, and therefore better trail conditions, than the Colins expedition had experienced in 1830. But the true inspiration for the speed of their travel was the fear inspired by the threat of war with Black Hawk. The settlers returned to Fort Dearborn in a panic, carrying very little with them, and seldom stopping to rest.

When the initial panic was over, the settlers realized they couldn't stay away from their land for long. If they missed the planting season, they would be out of provisions again for the coming winter. Some of the men from the Naper Settlement, who had accompanied their families to Fort Dearborn, returned to build a fort near their own homes. This new fort, which they named Fort Payne, would provide the settlers with protection in the future, so that they could stay close to home and tend to their own crops.

Chapter 13

As the war continued, Agatha went on gathering berries, hunting, and tending her garden. She kept her eyes open for trouble, and her gun and ammunition nearby, but she was not afraid. Her main concern now was that she was running low on the supplies she had so carefully husbanded. Her flour was long gone but the Indians had taught her to make corn meal. To make her boots last as long as possible, she had traded with the Indians for moccasins. Now she was running low on sugar and coffee, and she needed new boots.

Agatha knew she would soon have to go to the Naper trading post to replenish her supplies. She dreaded this. Over time, she had come to value her quiet, orderly life. So far, she had managed to avoid direct contact with the settlers. She was content just to talk to Sarah and to remember her home, so far away in Ireland. The people she'd encounter at the trading post would surely ask her all manner of questions. She preferred trading with the Indians who respected her privacy as she did theirs. Still, some chores in life were unavoidable, no matter how unpleasant. Agatha began preparing herself for the day she would have to make the trip into the Naper Settlement.

Early one summer morning, as the sun was coming up, Agatha awoke and prepared to start her day's chores. The cool breeze felt good as she gathered firewood from the woodpile by the hut. She brought it to the fire pit that she had dug in front of the hut for summer cooking. The hot embers of yesterday's fire ignited the wood she added now and started a fire she could cook with all day. Next, Agatha took her coffee pot and filled it with water and then added roasted, ground coffee beans. She suspended the coffee pot from a pole that was supported on each end of the fire pit by forked sticks she had lodged in the ground.

While the coffee was heating, Agatha prepared her breakfast of corn meal mush. This was made from corn she had crushed in a mortar and now mixed with water, sugar, and cinnamon. When the coffee was ready, she removed the pot from the fire and placed a frying pan, which had legs and a long handle, directly on the fire. To this pan she added water. Once the water had come to a boil, Agatha slowly added her corn meal mixture, stirring constantly until the mush was thick and smooth. She could eat some of this with her coffee now. The rest she would set aside to cool. For her mid-day meal, she could slice up the cold mush and fry it with fish.

Stooping over the pit to cook her meal was always hard on Agatha's back. She had thought she would get used to this eventually, but it never got easier. Agatha carefully straightened up and slowly arched her back in an effort to ease the pain. Then, after placing some mush in a bowl and pouring coffee into a tin cup, Agatha went over to Sarah's grave to visit while she ate. There was no milk for her mush, but Agatha would let it cool off before tasting it and would take frequent sips of coffee to wash it down. Milk would have made this a better meal, but she liked it well enough.

"Well Sara," said Agatha softly, "I have enough fish for my mid-day meal and supper. I may even dry some to eat later. I traded with Bear Hunter yesterday. He gave me some of the fish they had caught the night before. It takes me a long time to catch fish alone. I can only stand on the river bank with my pole in the water and wait. The Indians can catch a lot at night, using torches to lure the fish to the water's surface where they can be speared. I needed a new rawhide covering for the door of the hut as well. For the fish and the rawhide, I gave Bear Hunter two embroidered pillow cases. He liked the embroidery and wanted it to add to his clothing. I am curious to see how he uses them."

Agatha paused to eat as a cardinal appeared from the trees and hopped around on the ground in search of food. "Look at the colorful birds here, Sarah!" said Agatha. "I used to watch them when I went walking in the countryside at home." Agatha finished her breakfast and sat quietly thinking to herself. The warmth of the sun on her face, and the sweet sound of the birds, soothed her. She forgot where she was for a while and went back in her mind to Ireland. She pictured herself returning home from an afternoon walk. "Oh how sweet it will be to see Mother's face again," she thought, but the memory was no longer clear. "I wonder if Mother is still there?" she said aloud. Then reality came rushing back to her. "Probably not," said Agatha, as she rose with effort from Sarah's grave. "Mother was so old when I left and her heart was weak. Still, I wish I could see her now."

Agatha shook thoughts of Ireland from her head as she dusted off her clothing. "I asked Bear Hunter if there was a priest or a minister at the settlement yet, but he said no. With so many people there, surely a priest will join them soon." Picking up her dishes, Agatha returned to the fire. It was time to clean up and get on with her day.

One evening later in the summer, Agatha stood by the door of her hut and watched as Shattee walked off through the deep prairie grass. She enjoyed his visits since he brought news of the settlers as well as the

Indians and she could find out what was happening in the settlement near her without having to go there. But he had come this day to bring her more news of Black Hawk's war.

Things had been quiet for a while after the war started. The faint sounds of building and other day-to-day noises from the settlement faded as the settlers in the area hurried off to Chicago to find safety at Fort Dearborn. Agatha knew that Shattee's people kept in touch with Black Hawk and had occasion to visit many of the forts in Illinois. They were in a good position to bring back word to their own clans about the behavior of the white settlers and Black Hawk's warriors. Shaking her head at what she'd just heard, Agatha walked over to Sarah's grave and, sitting down, she repeated what Shattee had told her.

"Shattee told me that settlers all over Illinois have left their homes and headed for the safety of the forts. Some people, in their panic, even left sick and crippled family members behind. Far from here, some Potawatomi found an old man who was bed-ridden alone in his home. He was left there by his family when they hurried to a fort! Fortunately for him, the Indians stayed with him and took care of him until some of his family returned. Imagine their surprise and shame. They must have expected to find a dead man."

Agatha thought for a while, trying to put herself in that family's shoes. She thought of the horror stories these people must have heard that could make them so afraid they would betray an old man. "Perhaps they heard about the miller who hated the Indians and always treated them badly," said Agatha, trying to understand the panic of the settlers. "According to Shattee, one of the Potawatomi warned the miller and his neighbors to seek shelter at a fort, but the miller refused to leave his home. He even convinced some of his neighbors to stay on their land and work at his mill. It seems Black Hawk's men raided the area and killed every man, woman and child, except for two young girls they took captive. Stories like that could create a lot of panic," said Agatha, still not comprehending how anyone could leave their loved ones alone to face such a fate. Agatha began to clear away some grass and weeds from around Sarah's grave as she continued to tell Sarah the latest news about Black Hawk and his followers.

"Shattee said that fear caused some settlers to leave their own children behind! Today he told me about a couple who had to ford a river to reach safety. They accidentally left one of their children, a toddler, on the far bank. The man would have gone back for his daughter, but his wife told him to leave the child behind, she was in such a panic to get to the fort. That poor child! Fortunately, some neighbors found the child and took her to the fort with them."

Agatha had been bewildered to hear stories of cruelty and kindness exhibited by both the Indians and the settlers. "I guess you never know who the enemy really is," she said, thanking God that she had never experienced such panic in her own life. "Imagine, Sarah," she said, "what must it be like to hate so much that you could kill strangers? But worst of all, how can anyone be so afraid as to leave family members behind to such a fate; especially, the poor, helpless children?"

"We are not in as much danger here, Sarah. Shattee told me that Black Hawk's men seem to be concentrating on large settlements or the more prosperous settlers. When they find a home that has been abandoned, his warriors sometimes leave the home standing, but destroy everything in it. They believe the returning settlers will be terrified if they approach their homes thinking they were untouched and then find them destroyed inside. I guess they think this will make the settlers give up and leave for good."

Agatha stopped fussing around the grave and sat quietly for a while, lost in thought. As she sat there, she began to absentmindedly rub her jaw. Finally, the aching of a tooth pushed its way into her thoughts and Agatha roused herself. Slowly, she got up and turned back towards the hut to start fixing her supper, but paused when she remembered something else. "Oh yes," she said, turning back to the grave. "Shattee told me that the people in the settlement near us have returned from Chicago and are staying at a new fort here; Fort Payne, I think he called it. He has offered to take me there if I wish, but I don't want the noise and it would be too far away from you."

That said, Agatha returned to her hut to begin meal preparations. She glanced over at the gun that she kept propped up by the door. "If trouble comes," Agatha said to herself, "I will fight with everything I have, with the iron skillet if necessary, but I will not leave my Sarah."

Months passed, and the Black Hawk war raged on. A man was killed near the new fort, but Agatha neither heard nor saw any sign of the warriors. Early one morning, Agatha finished her breakfast and went to gather corn from the garden. She was not long at her work when a fine rain began to fall. Agatha looked up towards the heavens and let the rain fall softly on her face as she breathed in the fragrant smell of the trees and her garden and the earth as it became wet. For a while she forgot the pain of rheumatism in her back and the dull ache from her teeth. As she stood there, eyes closed, the image of a green Irish hillside came into her mind, and it felt as if time had stood still for a few precious moments.

Sometimes, when a moment like this came, she would find renewed energy to complete her tasks; pretending all the while that she was a young girl again, doing her chores, and that Mother and Father would soon be home for dinner. If her reverie produced feelings of loneliness, she shook them off saying, "That will do now, Agatha. You have no time for tears." She would follow up these stern words with vigorous exercise such as chopping wood, or digging up a new section for her garden. She would never go fishing then, where time would pass slowly and such thoughts could steal up and overtake her, undermining her efforts to survive and stay put until a priest could be found for Sarah.

But today, before she could stay too long in her reverie, she felt a presence nearby that brought her back to reality. She opened her eyes and turned to see Shattee standing quietly, watching her.

Chapter 14

Black Hawk finally surrendered at harvest time, and word spread quickly to Shattee's people. Shattee set out early the following morning to tell Left Alone Woman that the war was at an end. He approached her campsite on foot and saw her standing in the garden, her face turned skyward as a gentle rain fell. As he looked at her, he thought how she had changed since he first saw her with the expedition so many seasons ago.

Her hair, once the color of a prairie fire at night, was now the color of snow. Her plump, muscular figure had become lean, but he could still see muscle, like ropes, on her arms when her shirtsleeves were rolled up. When Left Alone Woman was with the expedition, she had worn a dress and stood erect with just the slightest rounding of her shoulders. Now, she wore men's pants, which were gathered at the waist and held up with rope. Her back had developed a pronounced curve and her skin, once smooth and pale, was weathered and lined from exposure to the sun and wind. Her body had been changed, but her spirit had not been broken. Left Alone Woman's voice was still soft and warm whenever he came upon her speaking to Sarah at her graveside. Her gaze was still steady when she negotiated with Shattee's people. But when she stood, dreaming, a smile would come to her lips that softened the lines on her face.

When he came upon her like this, Shattee usually turned and quietly left her in peace. But today he was bringing important news, so he moved closer and waited for her to feel his presence. When she turned, startled at seeing him, he paused a moment longer and then spoke, "The war is over. Black Hawk has surrendered." Left Alone Woman only nodded. He saw tears forming in her eyes and knew she could not speak. Knowing she would not want him to see her cry, Shattee turned quickly and left her to her thoughts.

Chapter 15

Another harvest season was coming to an end. Agatha had gathered the last of her corn, squash and beans. Whenever possible, she'd gathered wild berries and nuts to supplement her diet. The Indians had taught her a great deal about making her food last throughout the winter. Over the summer, as her corn ripened, she'd eaten some of it immediately and then boiled, roasted and dried the rest for use in her cooking later. She had also dried and saved some of the berries and beans.

Inside the hut, Agatha looked over her supplies. She'd long since pulled one of the discarded chests from the expedition into the hut. Into this chest, she'd placed the food she had prepared for winter, along with the remaining supplies from her days with the expedition. "If I had panicked and run when Black Hawk's war started," she thought, "I would not have any food stored now." But looking closely at her other supplies, Agatha knew she still had a problem. She'd used the last of her coffee several days before, and her sugar supply was perilously low. It was time to go to the trading post in the settlement, but how she dreaded it! Agatha had known that she'd have to make the trip there someday, so she had collected pelts from the animals she'd trapped. There were bound to be many questions asked of her, and she would certainly be stared at. She was a stranger after all; and even more bizarre, a woman in men's clothing.

"No. I must not wear my husband's clothes into the settlement," Agatha thought. "That would surely cause trouble." Agatha rummaged through her own old chest in which she kept her personal belongings. At last, she found what she was looking for: her good Sunday dress. It was purple cotton with a white lace collar. Her mother had made her the collar long ago and Agatha had taken special care to attach it to each new dress she made for church over the years. The dress was plain otherwise, with long sleeves and a full, long skirt. It seemed so heavy and bulky compared to her husband's shirts and pants.

As she contemplated her change of clothing, Agatha realized she would also have to do something with her hair. She had given up her habit of combing her hair each night once the expedition was forced to stop and take care of the sick. She kept her hair as clean as she could, always washing it when she bathed in the river, but it was no longer soft and shiny. It was white, wiry, and often badly tangled. She gave it a peremptory brushing in the morning and then left it alone until the next day. In the winter, she would pull it back and tie it in place so that it added protection for the back of her neck from the wind and snow. In the heat of summer, she would often stick her hair up under her hat so that any breeze that blew might cool her. But this would not do today. She'd have to find her hairpins and combs, and then work at taming her hair before she dared go to the trading post.

It took time for Agatha to locate what she needed. The pins and combs were wrapped in a linen handkerchief near the bottom of the chest. She even found her hand mirror, long forgotten near the bottom of the trunk. As she pulled the mirror out, Agatha caught a glimpse of herself in it. "Mother!" she cried out before realizing it was her own image she saw. She was in worse shape than she'd thought. The reflection she saw in the water as she bathed had been much more forgiving. Agatha took a long look into the mirror. As she did this, she placed her hand upon her cheek and marveled at how lined her face had become. She looked over her hair. There was no red left; it was snow white as her mother's had been when she'd last seen her in Ireland.

Then Agatha noticed that her lips had acquired the same bluish tinge that her mother's had had. "I have Dropsy," she thought, "just like Mother. What a funny sounding name for such a serious illness. I remember Mother's heart was failing and she was often tired and short of breath those last few years we lived with her. No wonder I am having trouble doing my chores. I get breathless now just like she did."

After placing the mirror, face down, at the bottom of the chest, Agatha covered it over with her other belongings. She put her purple dress and the handkerchief containing the hairpins and combs on top of the pile. "I need no mirror to help me dress," she said as she gently lowered the lid of the chest. "I will walk to the trading post another day. Now, I must go hunting."

Agatha stood up from her kneeling position by the side of the chest and, for the first time, she realized how much more difficult it was for her to straighten up. "I must be careful, for there is no one here to care for me if I get sick," she thought. She knew the Indians had many strange medicines that they used but she doubted they could do anything for her. "There is no medicine for old age," she said aloud, still amazed at the sight she had just seen in the mirror. "I must rest when I get out of breath," she thought. "It may take me longer to do my chores, but I am in no hurry."

Putting on her husband's old coat, she walked over to the doorway of her hut, then she paused for a moment to look back at her surroundings. "There is nowhere for me to go anyway," she said. With that, she stepped outside and headed for the traps she had laid some distance from the hut.

A few weeks later, Agatha knelt down to rummage through her cedar chest. She was looking for her husband's best shirt, which she'd promised to Shattee in return for coffee and maple sugar. She was so relieved! Not long ago, she'd been trying to prepare herself for the unhappy day when she would have to go into the settlement for supplies. Now the two items that were so essential to her were being offered in trade by Shattee.

She'd been hunting early in the morning when she encountered him. He told her that the people of his village would be moving across the Mississippi now that gathering time was over. They would spend their time hunting and locating the best spot to start a garden when planting season came again. Now that Black Hawk's war was over, the leaders of the remaining tribes in the area were being strongly encouraged by government agents to sell their land and move further west. The Potawatomi leaders believed that soon the soldiers would force them to go, so they wanted to find a good location for their village now. They needed a spot that would be good for hunting and fishing as well as gardening; but they knew that the first time they prepared and planted the new land, they would not get as much food as they needed. Some of his people would stay on at the new village when next planting season came, but others would have to return then to plant in soil they knew would bring them a great deal of food.

Agatha admired their farsightedness. "They should do well by planning so far ahead," she thought. But their plans also meant that she would not have them much longer as trusted trading partners. She was accustomed to them moving around for a few months at a time as they prepared sugar, for instance, but she was not used to them being gone for very long. It had never occurred to her that they would move on. Some of them, Shattee included, were the only friends she had. She would miss them and the news they brought her.

Still trying to grasp the effect that their move would have on her life, Agatha had been startled when Shattee asked what she planned to do. He'd wondered if she wanted him to escort her back to Chicago, but she had shaken her head to that offer. Then he'd asked if she wanted to move to the nearby settlement. Her response had been an emphatic, "No!" but she'd known that her attitude was unrealistic. It was going to be very difficult for her to live entirely on her own. At the very least, she would have to go into the settlement for some supplies soon. Then Shattee had come to her rescue once more, asking if there was anything she needed before his people moved on.

"My coffee and sugar are gone," she'd said. "Have you any to trade? I can give you my husband's best Sunday shirt in exchange." Agatha had been pretty sure that Shattee would want the shirt since the Indians were wearing more of the white men's clothing, especially when they served as guides for the soldiers and the settlers. Shattee had agreed to the trade and promised to bring the sugar and coffee to Agatha before his people left.

At last, Agatha found what she was looking for. Still kneeling, she pulled out the shirt, unfolded it, and held it up in front of her to make sure it was undamaged after long storage in the chest. The shirt was in fine shape, but of course it should be, since it was last worn for Sarah's christening. That day, so long ago, her husband had said that he would not wear the shirt again until they celebrated the first Sunday in their own home in America.

Slowly lowering the shirt to her lap, Agatha thought of how happy he had been in Ireland. He'd had his dreams then and his clear blue eyes had held such sparkle when at last they'd set sail for America. Poor man; he was so bitterly disappointed by their life in New York. He was never truly happy again, until the day he knew for certain they would take part in the Colins Expedition. Then, for the last time, Agatha saw the once familiar look of excitement on his face, and in his eyes. "All that dreaming, and he never saw anything he ever wanted come true here," she said aloud, slowly shaking her head.

Agatha gathered the shirt to her chest and, bending her head down, began to cry quietly, rocking gently back and forth as she did so. She cried as she thought of Ireland and her parents, the young man she'd married, the children who were gone. She cried for everyone she'd lost, and would lose now. So lost in misery, she didn't notice the shadows grow across the floor of her hut.

When she awoke, shivering, it was night. At some point, she must have sat down, leaning more on her left hip, with her legs pushed out to one side and her left arm resting on the edge of the open chest. The shirt, still clutched in her right hand, was resting on her left hip. Her neck felt so stiff and sore as she moved her head carefully and looked around the room.

It was very dark in the hut. The fire in the center of the room was barely more than embers now. She must do something about that! She'd forgotten to build it up, forgotten even to make supper. She was hungry now and chilled to the bone. Agatha took the shirt and placed it in the open chest before trying to straighten her upper body and stand up. She felt so stiff! With great difficulty, Agatha turned herself until she was on her knees. Then she placed both hands on the edge of the open chest and slowly forced herself up into a standing position.

Her movements were awkward. It seemed to take forever before she was truly erect and able to walk slowly towards the door. She fumbled in the darkness until she located the small pile of wood that she had placed there to build up the fire for supper. Agatha moved back to the center of the room with her wood and placed it into the fire pit with great care, so as not to smother what little fire remained. Slowly, she coaxed the embers until the new firewood began to burn. She stood there for a moment, trying to decide what to do next. Although she was very hungry, she was far too cold to make supper. Instead, Agatha made her way to her bed along one wall of the hut. She lay down, covering herself with her blankets and pulled her knees up to her chest for added warmth. She lay shivering for a long time, until at last she fell asleep.

When Agatha awoke the next morning, she was hungry and sore. It took her a while to move her stiff body into a sitting position on the edge of her bed. Slowly, she leaned forward and placed her elbows on her knees, then she rested her forehead in her upraised hands. Thinking back over the events of the previous night, Agatha was appalled at how she'd let her sad feelings take over.

"I must not let this happen again," she thought, as she counted her sins of the night before. She had almost let the fire go out. She had waited too long to prepare supper and had to go to bed hungry and cold. Instead of thanking God for helping her stay here and take care of Sarah's grave, she had cried about things that were long gone.

"What a waste of precious time!" Agatha said aloud. "I must take better care of myself or I will not be around when a priest finally comes; and no one will know about my Sarah."

Resolving to make better use of her time in the future, she stood up and went out to gather firewood so she could cook her breakfast. Looking at the woodpile, she realized that she must add to it soon. "Not soon. Today," Agatha said with determination. "I must be sure I am prepared for winter. Today I shall chop wood and tonight, after it is all stacked and I have eaten supper, I shall go to bed early. Tomorrow, I can rise before the sun and do some fishing. God willing, I shall catch some fine fish to salt for winter." Agatha felt more hopeful now that she had made some plans. She gathered her wood and went back to the hut. At the doorway, she paused and looked back in the direction of Sarah's grave. "I cannot stop to chat today, Sarah," she said, "There will be time soon." Then she turned her back on the small, silent grave and went into the hut to prepare breakfast.

Chapter 16

When Shattee approached Left Alone Woman's wigwam that day, he could hear the slow and steady 'thwack' of someone chopping wood in the nearby grove. Following the direction of the sound, he came upon Left Alone Woman working with more energy than he had seen in her in a long time. He watched until she had finished cutting down a tree and then he moved forward to speak to her.

The woman, pausing from her work to take in great gulps of air, turned as Shattee approached. She wiped her brow with the back of her hand. "Afternoon," she said as she expelled another deep breath.

Shattee only nodded once, slowly, as he looked at her. Left Alone Woman's eyes shone with spirit, but her face looked gray and her lips were a terrible dark color. He had seen this before. Sometimes, the old ones in his tribe would recover their youthful strength for a short time before it left them forever. It was sad to see this in Left Alone Woman. "This will be the last time we meet," he thought. The silence stayed between them a moment longer as she caught her breath and he silently said good-bye to a friend.

"Have you come to trade now?" she asked, finally looking at the small bark basket and the cloth bag that he held.

"Yes," he said, adding, "We leave tomorrow when the sun rises."

"Come with me then," she said, leading the way back to her dwelling. When they reached her doorway, she lay down the ax and went inside to get her husband's shirt. Shattee stood outside, waiting. As he waited, he looked around the campsite and saw that there was very little remaining of the discards from her people. What Left Alone Woman had not used herself, or traded with his people, had been destroyed by animals and bad weather. Aside from the barrel that she kept by the wigwam for collecting rain, only a few wooden boxes remained. Shattee put the sugar and coffee beans down on one of the wooden boxes and went over to look into the barrel. It was half filled with water, which would save her some trips to the spring. That was one way she could save her strength. "Left Alone Woman has much to do to live through the snow time alone," he thought.

Shattee went back to the box where the coffee and maple sugar lay. The sugar was his payment for the shirt. The coffee really belonged to her, although she did not know it. It had been given to him long ago by her departing friends. He had agreed to return her to Fort Dearborn, when she was ready, in return. To spare her pride, she was never to be told of the trade. Shattee had stored the beans, waiting for the day he could complete his part of the bargain, but since she never went back to the fort, the beans belonged to her. To settle this dilemma honorably, he hoped that she would think the beans were part of a fair trade for the shirt. Left Alone Woman would need both the sugar and the coffee, along with all the food she could gather herself, to help her through the snow time.

By now, it was clear that the woman could not continue much longer on her own. The Potawatomi had watched her struggle to stay near her daughter in spite of severe weather, her physical deterioration, and her dwindling food supplies. Help was certainly available at the settlement, which was now growing and thriving. They would not tell anyone of her existence, however, since the settlers might try to interfere with her choices. Left Alone Woman had faced her struggles with dignity and courage. She was as brave as any warrior, and entitled to choose the way her life journey would end.

The woman came out carrying the folded shirt in her hands. She laid it carefully down beside the coffee and sugar on the wooden box. Then, after examining the contents of the cloth bag and the bark container, she looked very pleased and said, "So much coffee and sugar; now I will not have to go into the trading post!"

Shattee, in turn, unfolded the shirt and held it up. He could see that it was well made and hoped that she would not realize that the amount of maple sugar he had given her was itself worth the shirt.

"I made that shirt myself, in Ireland," she said.

Shattee had never understood where Ireland was, but he nodded and, holding the shirt in one hand, said, "It is a good trade."

Left Alone Woman smiled and offered to make him some coffee, but he asked for water instead, knowing she would need to keep her supplies for the snow time. They talked for a while longer about the journey his people would be making, and about the work she must get done before the snow fell. When it was time to go, Shattee said he would be returning with some of his people at planting time.

"I will still be here," Left Alone Woman said with a smile. But Shattee did not believe that she would. Her only chance was to go to the settlement and he knew she would not do that. Shattee took one last look at her and he left. There was much to be done at his village and nothing more he could do here.

Chapter 17

The winter that began in 1832 had been even harder on Agatha. The energy she'd found in the fall, to replenish her wood supply and to catch and salt fish, had vanished. Agatha had become increasingly short of breath when she set about her chores. Over time, she fell behind on hunting, and had used up most of her reserve food supply by winter's end.

Now that Shattee and his people were so far away, she no longer had any news about what was happening at the settlement. Not that it really mattered. To her, the settlers were unwelcome outsiders who had failed to provide her with the one thing in life she desired most: a priest to pray over Sarah's grave. She doubted that a priest would move into the area in the middle of winter, so there was really no reason to let the settlers find out she lived nearby. Knowing the Indians were not available to trade with, and wanting to avoid going to the settlement's trading post, she gave herself ever-smaller rations of food.

Agatha knew her health was rapidly deteriorating. Aside from the shortness of breath, her jaw ached all of the time and there was a nasty taste in her mouth due to a bad back tooth. She knew that the tooth was infected, but she was unable to pull it out. Several of her teeth had grown loose and fallen out during the winter, but this sore one remained stubbornly anchored in her jaw.

Her inadequate diet and failing health made Agatha less able to tolerate the cold weather. She spent most of her time now huddled by the fire or making brief trips to Sarah's grave. As a result, the wood supply that should have lasted her through the winter was used up too soon.

At last, it was spring and Agatha knew that Shattee and some of his people would soon be returning. If she could make her supplies last until they returned, she believed that everything would be all right. But she was having trouble concentrating, and this was interfering with her hunting. Several times during the winter, she'd lost track of where she'd set her traps, or she would absentmindedly check the same ones several times and neglect others. Agatha had hoped that her memory and strength would improve with the weather, but that hadn't happened this year.

Each day, she rose and went out in search of firewood to keep her warm for the day and to cook her breakfast the following morning. Since freshly cut wood was difficult to burn, she gathered the dead branches from the trees in the nearby groves. As time went on, she had to go further afield to find them. Agatha was rising later each day now, so the struggle to find and haul back the wood she needed occupied most of the remaining daylight hours.

On this particular spring day, when she went outside to bring in the remains of the branches needed to cook her morning breakfast, she was shocked to realize she had slept 'til midday. "No wonder I am so hungry," she thought. Then, looking down at the few twigs remaining in the woodpile, she realized that there wasn't enough left to heat her morning meal. Thinking, "I must eat or I will not be able to do my chores," Agatha looked around her for an answer to her problem. "Of course," she said aloud, "I can use those old boxes that were left here by the expedition." Agatha fetched her ax from the hut and set to work breaking up enough of the wood to make her breakfast fire. This was much easier than chopping and hauling wood from the groves. When at last she had the fire going, she set about making a pot of coffee. She had been rationing coffee, so it tasted weak at the beginning of the day. However, she kept the pot on the fire whenever she worked around the hut, knowing that, by the end of the day, the coffee would taste thick and strong.

Once the coffee was ready, she looked at the supplies in her chest and decided just to eat a piece of hardtack and save her other food for a later time. She dipped the hardtack in the coffee to soften it for the sake of her sore and loose teeth, but it still seemed to take a long time to consume her miserable breakfast.

Agatha stepped outside to face the day's chores. She walked over to Sarah's grave and knelt down to speak to her daughter for a few moments. "Well Sarah," she said, as lightly as she could, "your Mother has gotten herself into a mess. The rain barrel is nearly empty, so I must make several trips each day to the stream with my bucket. It is not very far from here, but it takes me so long to get there and back lately. My pantry is getting very bare also. I have a bit of hardtack left, but I cannot make more since my remaining flour is very wormy. I have eaten all of the salt fish and have not done any fishing to replace it. I cannot remember when I last checked my traps, either."

Looking around, her eyes came to rest on the fire pit she had long since abandoned in front of the hut. "I will be glad when I feel warm enough to cook outside again," she said. "The smell of meat cooking on the fire in the hut can make the air so heavy and sour." She paused for a while, thinking of nothing in particular, then she shook her head and wondered aloud, "What have I been doing with my days? I am so tired by bedtime, but I seem to get so little done."

She struggled to her feet, and then looked down at the grave again. The cross she had made for it had been blown apart during a winter storm and she still had not replaced it. "I shall make a cross for you later today, my dear," Agatha said. "But first, I must see if I have snared any game and then I must break up the rest of the wooden boxes I have here."

Her attempt to check her traps took all afternoon. She was having difficulty remembering where she had set them. Late in the day, she returned to her hut with two scrawny rabbits. "Well," she said, holding up the rabbits as she paused by the grave to catch her breath, "this is not much but it is all I could find today. I must be careful to cook these in a thick gravy or eat them with cornmeal mush. Shattee told me spring rabbits are so lean, you can starve yourself if you eat them alone. Now I must build the fire up to cook them. I am so hungry!"

Agatha walked towards her hut and then realized that she hadn't cut up any firewood since breakfast. Her shoulders drooped as she thought of what she still had to do before she could eat her dinner. She lay the rabbits down on one of the boxes outside her hut and went in to get her ax. Coming outside again, she realized she didn't have the energy left to break up the wood. "Perhaps," she thought, "if I sit down and prepare the rabbits first, I will feel rested enough to break up the wood I need to build up the fire."

It was well after dark when Agatha stepped out of her hut carrying the cooked rabbits. She walked over to the grave and said, "I shall just sit here with you while I eat the rabbits. I am too hungry to fuss over cornmeal mush now. When I have finished with this meat, I shall cook and eat the mush."

154

Agatha sat down by Sarah's grave and started eating. The meat was very tough and hard to chew since rabbits have no extra fat on their bones by spring. "Like me," she thought, looking down at her own thin body. "Look at how I am shrinking away. I have not been this thin since I was a young girl. At home, Mama would have cooked us a fine rabbit stew with lots of potatoes and a thick slab of bread and butter for each of us. That would make a fine Sunday dinner. Afterwards, we might even have some warm pie."

As she continued to chew on the meat, her gums started bleeding. "This has been happening a lot lately," she thought. To spare herself further pain, Agatha took a sharp knife and cut the meat into chunks that she could swallow. When she'd finished eating the rabbit, she sat looking far away. In her mind's eye, she could see her mother's table laid out for Sunday dinner, and smell all of the delicious aromas coming out of the kitchen. "It was so warm in our cottage," she remembered. "After dinner I would play with the rag doll Mother made for me, until it was time for bed." She sat for a long time thinking of the happy times she'd had as a young girl in Ireland. She pictured herself playing with her young friends on the hills near her home. Then she thought of the times she would sit quietly in a corner of the room as neighbors gathered in her parents' home. It would be past her bedtime, but, as long as she remained quiet, the adults would forget she was there as they enjoyed each other's company.

Her thoughts wandered far and wide over the events of her childhood, but always they returned to the warm hearth of her long lost home. She remembered quietly trying to pour herself a cup of warm cider while her parents were engaged in conversation with their company. But the jug was too heavy and made a terrible racket when she tried to set it back down on the table. Hearing the noise, her mother had remembered her then and called out to her, "Agatha, time to go to bed now my girl." The sound of her mother's voice was so clear in her mind that Agatha was startled from her reverie, even as she answered aloud, "Yes, Mama."

The cold night air brought an end to her happy thoughts as she struggled to get herself back up on her feet. Shivering, Agatha hurried back to the hut and climbed into her bed, pulling the covers close to her chin. She struggled to remember something important that she was supposed to do tonight. What was it? Her mind slowly went over the events of the day, but her memory was foggy now and she gave up the effort. Still, it nagged at her, in the back of her mind, as she slowly gave in and fell asleep.

Agatha's sleep that night was fitful. In spite of her exhaustion, her sleep was disturbed by her stomach that ached from trying to digest unchewed chunks of spring rabbit. When she finally struggled to get up the next day, she felt as though she had been at work all night long. Then she remembered what had been in the back of her mind the night before. "Of course!" she thought, "I should not have eaten that rabbit without some fried cornmeal mush."

She looked over to the center of the room at the fire that had burned down to a few flickering embers. It seemed to her that the fire struggled harder to stay alive each day. She had to spend more and more time feeding it wood and coaxing it back into flames. There was so little life left in it now, she would have to bring some wood in quickly to save what remained of the fire and build it up so that she could cook her breakfast.

With this in mind, Agatha went over to the chest to get her jacket. But laying over the top of the chest were her nightgown and shawl. Looking down at herself, she realized that she was still wearing her work clothes and coat. "How long has it been since I have even changed?" she wondered. "I had better bathe myself and air out these clothes," she thought. Then her stomach ache began anew and she decided that she must eat before she did anything else.

When she stepped outside to gather firewood, Agatha looked up at the position of the sun in the sky and realized that it was already afternoon. She went in the direction of the woodpile, but there was no wood left. She had not cut any extra wood yesterday as she had planned. Agatha fetched her ax and walked over to the remnants of the boxes, they would have to do for now. She cut and pulled the wood apart and took it inside to start her breakfast fire. It was touch and go, but she finally managed to get the fire burning again.

By mid afternoon, Agatha was outside sitting by Sarah's grave. She felt a little better now that she had consumed the cornmeal mush, but she knew that there was almost no food left in the chest in her hut. She was drinking the last of her coffee as she sat trying to organize her thoughts. "I have so much to do today, Sarah. I just do not have enough time to get it done before dark. I feel so different now. It gets harder to keep going each day. I fear I may never get a priest for you, my dear daughter, but at least someone must know that you are here. Someone must know you existed."

Agatha looked at the stub of the cross that still poked out of the ground on Sarah's grave. "I promised I would make you a new cross and I will do that now before I start anything else. At least I can accomplish that quickly," said Agatha as she struggled to her feet. She looked around by the hut for some twigs, but there was nothing left. She went inside the hut to see what she could use and her eyes fell on the chest where she kept her clothing. All she had left was this chest and the one in which she stored food. "I can leave the clothes on the ground," she said to herself.

She opened the chest and started to pull her clothes out when she saw the purple dress that she had set aside for a trip into the settlement. "I know I must go there soon, but I am so dirty now." Agatha struggled out of her coat. She would not try to bathe in the river; it was too light out and the water was too cold. There was no water left in her bucket; she had used that to make her coffee. "Perhaps there is some water left in the rain barrel," she thought. Taking the dipper from her water bucket, Agatha walked outside to check the barrel. Reaching in to get the remaining water from the bottom of the barrel, she lost her balance. As she fell, she pulled the barrel over too.

Struggling to her knees, she saw that the last of the water was pouring out. Agatha scooped up what she could of the water that was streaming out, but it did little more than wet her hands. She ran her hands over her face as though she were splashing the water on and scrubbing her face with it. She dipped her hands back into the barrel for another scoop of water, and repeated the process of patting her hands against her face once again. Thinking that she was scooping up great quantities of water, Agatha continued this process for a short time, but all that she accomplished was to streak more dirt down her cheeks. "There," she said at last, "That is much better."

Agatha went back into the hut and pulled off her boots, pants and shirt, and then struggled into her purple dress. The dress, which was now much too big for her, hung on her shrunken frame and the weight of it seemed to drag her down. She looked down at her boots again, thinking to put them on, but they were in tatters. She had held them together this past winter with strips of cloth, but nothing would hold them on now. "I shall find my old shoes and wear them," she thought, heading back to the chest.

Then she saw her hairbrush and pins sitting on the pile of clothing still in the chest. "I must fix my hair before going to the trading post. Mama would never have permitted me to go into town without first making sure I was neat and clean, with my hair freshly brushed."

Agatha attempted to pull the brush through her hair, but it was difficult because her hair was so tangled and dirty. Her arms grew tired quickly as she struggled with the brush, until at last she gave up and put the brush down. Gathering her long hair between her hands, she twisted it up in some semblance of a bun and stuck her hairpins into it. Some of the hair she had failed to gather up hung down her back, but she didn't notice this. Now completely exhausted and out of breath, Agatha staggered to her bed and sprawled across it, falling asleep immediately. Her dreams were a tangle of memories from her life.

At first, she dreamed of herself as a young girl and then it was Sarah's face she saw on her own small body. She was happy now. She and Sarah were safe at home in Ireland. She was taking Sarah outside with her as she gathered peat for the fire. It was cold outside and she was shivering, but Sarah was laughing and wanting to play. The cold didn't seem to bother young Sarah at all.

The two, mother and child, joined hands and danced in a circle, singing a song whose words Agatha could not quite hear. In her joy, Agatha swung her daughter up into her arms and held her. But Sarah's head dropped back and Agatha could see that she was dead.

With a start, Agatha woke up. Her horrible circumstances came back to her in a rush. She sat up, remembering now that she had promised to make a new cross for Sarah's grave. She looked around for some wood to use and then remembered that she still hadn't cut any. Going over to the fire, Agatha selected a few sticks that had never burned. The fire, which she had not built as carefully as she should have, had finally gone out.

Agatha tore a strip from the tattered shirt she had worn yesterday and used that to hold the wood in the shape of a cross. She went to the door of the hut, cross in hand, but her dress, which was so large for her now, caught under her bare feet and she tripped and fell onto the ground outside. She lay there, stunned for a few minutes, the sound of her heart pounding in her ears, the cross lying close to her body. Her mind again carried her back to the safety of her parents' home. She was a young girl again, getting all dressed up. "Hurry, Agatha," she heard her mother calling to her, "It is time for you to go into town."

Her eyes focused on the ground around her. "I am ready to go now," she said, slowly getting to her feet. She staggered towards the settlement, tripping over her dress again and again until finally she gathered the front of it up into a ball in her arms. It was getting dark and she was unable to see the ground in front of her clearly. Her mouth was dry, but the pain in her stomach and the once constant pain in her jaw had faded. In fact, she really didn't feel much of anything anymore. Her bare feet were becoming bloody from sharp twigs and small, jagged branches that she walked on, but Agatha was oblivious to this.

She was just a few hundred yards from her hut when her foot caught on the exposed root of a tree and she fell forward, hitting her head soundly on a rock.

Chapter 18

When Shattee and his people returned for the spring planting, he found her. He and his hunting party had stopped at Left Alone Woman's hut to check on her and had found the area deserted. Shattee had hoped that she'd finally gone into the settlement for help, but in his heart he believed that she had not. They searched the area and found her remains not far from her hut where she'd fallen. Little more than some bits of hair and flesh clinging to bones, and the torn rags of her dress remained to testify to the damage done by the elements and animals to her dead body. There was so little left of her that Shattee decided to bury her where she lay.

It was a custom amongst the Potawatomi to bury their dead with their most valued possessions, so the hunting party returned to her hut and picked out her coffee and cooking pots along with the shovel they would need to dig her grave. As Shattee stepped out of the hut once more, he saw the freshly made cross laying on the ground near the door. This he also picked up and took back to Left Alone Woman's body. Shattee and the others dug her grave and placed her in it, along with the pots and Sarah's cross. Then they covered her over with a mound of dirt and topped this mound off with rocks and stones to protect what was left of her from the animals.

When the burial was complete, Shattee and his people returned to her hut and dismantled it. The Potawatomi tried never to waste anything, so they carried the pieces from her hut and everything else that remained away with them. Left Alone Woman would have no further use for these things and there was no sense in leaving anything to rot away, unused but useful.

Shattee lingered as the others rode off, and took one last look at the spot where Left Alone Woman had lived for so long. There was no longer any sign of her there. He would miss her, but at last her struggle was over. "Now your spirit can soar with the eagles," he said, looking up towards the white clouds in the sky. Then he turned and rode away.

SECTION 3

AGATHA'S JOURNEY THROUGH TIME

Chapter 19

Agatha rose from the ground after she had fallen. Although she'd hit her head hard, she felt no pain. She tried to gather her thoughts, to figure out what she had tripped on and how much time had gone by since she started out for the settlement. But she couldn't seem to grasp the concept of time clearly. She looked down to the spot where she had fallen and there lay the body of an old woman.

"Did I trip over her?" wondered Agatha as she leaned down to get a closer look. The remnants of a dress clung to the body. Because the dress was so badly torn, and mired by mud and rain, she was unable to determine its original color. "Poor woman, she must have lain here for days," thought Agatha, moving closer to see who this poor creature was. It was clear that the woman's body had been chewed by animals, but most of the flesh still remained. "She could not have been dead too long, though, or the animals would have cleaned all the meat off her bones," she said to herself. The thought of an animal attack made Agatha think about how careful she'd been, when burying Sarah, to place stones on top of the grave to protect her body from animals. As soon as Sarah entered her thoughts, Agatha found herself back at her hut, standing in front of Sarah's grave. This sudden change of scene confused her. She looked around the campsite, trying to figure out how she got there so quickly. As she looked around, Agatha was appalled at the chaos she had left behind. Bits of wood from the broken up barrels lay on the ground and close to the door of the hut lay the cross that she'd made to put on Sarah's grave. She walked over to the doorway and stooped down to pick the grave marker up off the ground.

"Strange. Bending down is not difficult anymore," she thought as she reached out to grasp the cross; but her hand went straight through it. She tried over and over again but her hand was unable to grip the wood. Agatha knelt on the ground and tried to make sense of what was happening. Each time she reached out for the cross, she tried to will it to appear in her hand. Night and day intermingled. Time meant nothing as she continued in her efforts to pick up the simple cross so she could place it on Sarah's grave.

Then Shattee appeared with Bear Hunter and other members of a hunting party. "They have returned at last!" Agatha said softly as she stood and hurried forward to greet her old friends. But Shattee ignored her and slowly walked around in front of the hut, examining the unkempt state of her camp. With a frown upon his face, Shattee stepped inside Agatha's hut uninvited. In a rage Agatha followed him, and stood before him, hands on her hips.

"Shattee," she said, indignantly, "how dare you come into my home without my permission!" But Shattee only looked about the room, his shoulders sagging slightly, as if in disappointment that he had not found whatever it was he was looking for.

Then she heard him say, "Left Alone Woman is gone. I hope she is safe." Having said that, he walked to the door and spoke to the others waiting outside.

"Who is this woman you are looking for?" demanded Agatha, hurrying after Shattee as he stepped outside. "And why are you ignoring me?" she added, but then she stopped as she realized that, although she had heard his words, Shattee had not opened his mouth to speak them.

"Did I read his thoughts?" she said, with awe. She reached up and ran her hand through her hair as she tried to make some sense out of what had been happening to her since her fall. Although she had struck her head hard, it did not hurt. Nothing hurt her, and she could not apparently be seen or heard by those around her. "None of this can be happening. I must be dreaming," she said, unable to think of another explanation. She looked around her again and realized that she was quite alone. The Indians, if they were ever with her, were gone.

"I wonder where Shattee is now," Agatha thought, and instantly she found herself standing beside him as he and the hunting party looked down at the old woman's body. Looking at the old woman, Agatha was horrified to see how little there was left of her now. "But that is not possible," she said. "I saw her only moments ago and there are no animals around here now. How could they have done so much damage, so fast, and then disappeared without a trace?"

The Indians were talking amongst themselves about someone they referred to as 'Left Alone Woman.' As Agatha listened to them, she realized that, although they were speaking their own language, she understood them. "This is amazing," she said to herself. "How can it be possible?"

At last, Shattee spoke up. "We must go back to her dwelling and gather her best tools for the burial. There is so little of her left, we shall bury her right here."

Agatha followed as they went back to her hut. It dawned on her at last that she was dead. "I am the one they call Left Alone Woman. It is my body they are burying today." She watched as Shattee went into her hut and selected several of her cooking tools to bury with her. As he stepped back out of the hut, Agatha went up to him and leaning close to his ear, she pleaded, "Pick up Sarah's cross. Pick it up and put it on her grave." Shattee stopped, looked down at the cross on the ground near his feet and stooped down to pick it up. He remained there for a few moments, examining the cross in his hand closely, and then looked around as though he'd heard something.

"At least Sarah shall have her marker," said Agatha triumphantly. Shattee stood up then and returned with the others to the body. He still held the cross in his hand. As they dug Agatha's grave she realized that if he had heard her message, he'd misunderstood it. Once the body and the other objects were laid in the grave, Shattee put the cross in too.

"No! No!" shouted Agatha, jumping into the grave to rescue the cross. But the Indians didn't hear her and proceeded to cover the body, and the cross, with dirt. The dirt fell through her onto the body as she vainly tried to pick up the cross. At last, she decided to stand beside Shattee again and try to stop the burial. As she shouted and gestured at him, the Indians finished filling in the grave and covered it with rocks. Agatha could feel Shattee's sadness as he stood looking at the grave once the burial process was complete. Then he and the others returned to the hut, dismantled it, and gathered everything of substance to take back with them to their own camp.

As the others were leaving, Shattee stayed behind briefly, to look over at the few scraps of wood and bark that were the remains of Agatha's camp. Then, he stood by the blackened pit that had once been her fire, and she could hear him thinking, "Good-bye Left Alone Woman." He looked up to the sky and said quietly, "May your spirit soar with the eagles."

"Good-bye my friend," Agatha said softly as she watched Shattee ride off. She looked around at the emptiness that had once been her home and at the unmarked grave she had guarded for three years. "I guess I truly am Left Alone Woman," she sighed, "For the Indians are gone now, and I must wait until I can tell someone about Sarah; no matter how long it takes."

Chapter 20

Agatha kept a close watch over her daughter's grave. All signs of it slowly disappeared as the indentation in the ground filled with leaves and debris. No longer aware of time as she had known it, she was only aware of the passage of events in the area around her, and came to appreciate the irony of her Indian name, Left Alone Woman. Once she had wanted to be left alone, but now that she so desperately wanted to contact passersby, she was utterly unable to make them see or hear her. She was not in heaven, nor was she in hell as she had learned these concepts in church. She was quite alone; but she didn't let this frighten her, for overriding everything else was the importance of her mission, her obsession: to make sure that people knew about her sweet Sarah. "They must bring a priest to her grave!" she thought. "Without a proper Christian burial, I have been left alone, out of Heaven. I must make sure that Sarah's soul is safe with God. Only a priest can do that."

She watched helplessly as people came and went, unknowingly trampling over Sarah's grave. Everyone was so caught up in their own cares, they didn't have time to notice the chill that surrounded them as Agatha came up to talk to them, nor did they understand the thoughts that she tried planting in their heads. In desperation, she did what she had refused to do in life; she went into the center of the settlement and tried to make contact with people on their own ground. To her dismay, she still could not make her presence felt, except to babies and small children whose responses to her went unnoticed by the adults around them.

"I know I was able to make Shattee hear part of my message about Sarah's cross when he was preparing to bury me," she thought. "But who can I find now who will hear my words?" Agatha decided to study the people in the settlement until she could identify one who could hear her and take Sarah's story to a priest.

Over time, she tried, without success, to communicate with some of the local residents. But she discovered that the townspeople were too preoccupied with their own plans and daily routines to notice her. Then, she heard the them talking about building the area's first Catholic church, so they wouldn't have to wait for a priest from Joliet to visit once a month. "I shall wait for the priest," she decided. "A man of God will surely be able to hear me. He can pray over Sarah's grave, and perhaps tell others about her."

By the mid 1840s, a small building had been erected to serve as the Catholic church and a priest was assigned to it. Agatha followed the priest as he went about visiting his new parishioners. She tried to speak to him when he sat quietly at night preparing his church services. It seemed that she was getting through to him; when she told him about Sarah's favorite Bible stories, he would go and open his Bible and read them. Finally, after testing his reactions a few more times, Agatha tried to lead him back to Sarah's grave.

First, she planted the idea in his head that it was a beautiful day for a walk; then, she directed him on the route to take which would lead to the graveside. The priest assumed the walk was a whim he'd had, and was receptive to Agatha's gentle directions. But, the walk was very frustrating for her because people constantly met up with the priest and would stop to chat with him.

"Say good-bye and walk on," Agatha would say to the priest again and again. She had never spoken to a Father like that in her life, but she was angry that he hadn't come sooner, while she was alive to show him Sarah's grave. Agatha berated the poor man as he unknowingly wasted time chatting with his parishioners. She realized that, though he didn't hear every word she said, he believed that her words were his own thoughts.

The daylight began to fade and they had not yet reached Sarah's grave. Agatha's discouragement deepened. The interruptions continued until, at last, she lost her temper. In great agitation, she shouted in the priest's ear, "It will soon be dark. This walk cannot go on forever. Say good-bye and go quickly!" Unfortunately for Agatha, her agitated state did get through to the priest and he found himself hurrying to end a conversation so that he could return to his rooms before dark. This was not what Agatha wanted to happen, but it was a valuable lesson to her about the power of strong emotions. Instead of communicating her destination to the priest, she had communicated her mood; he no longer felt in need of a leisurely walk with no clear destination.

"I must take better care to hold in my impatience the next time, for my anger did not help Sarah," said Agatha to herself. But there was not to be a next time. The priest was soon moved to another parish and the succession of priests who came after him did not hear her at all. At last, she gave up her hope of reaching a priest and returned to Sarah's graveside to wait for a better opportunity to tell her tale.

Thirty years passed. The Naper Settlement grew and was renamed the Village of Naperville. One day, Agatha heard the farmers in the area discussing civil war, and saw her opportunity to try again to reach the

173

living. By now, there were almost two thousand people living in the area and they prided themselves on the fact that hundreds of their young men were going off to fight. After thirty years of trying to communicate with local residents, she was prepared to leave the graveside in an effort to find a receptive person to hear her story.

"I cannot make anyone around Sarah's grave understand that she is buried here. People have been too busy to hear me; including the priests. No one will believe the children who do see me. Perhaps men who are about to go into battle will feel closer to God and will discover I am with them," she thought. With this new idea in mind, she followed some of the Naperville lads as they left to join the army.

When the young men first set off for the war, it was just an adventure in their minds and so they talked incessantly about it to each other. Agatha was unable to communicate with them through their excitement. But when they reached their destination, they saw the condition of the other soldiers, many of whom were in ragged clothing. The new recruits grew quiet and retreated into themselves. Agatha could hear their fearful thoughts as she visited each of the Naperville men in turn and tried to make her presence felt; but they mistook the chill that accompanied her presence for their own nervousness.

At last she realized that the new recruits were too afraid of dying to worry about anything else. She entered a nearby field hospital, where so many young men lay sick and wounded. "Perhaps, those who are near death will see me and will tell others when they get better." she thought. Agatha went from cot to cot, until at last she found a wounded soldier who looked up at her and knew that she was there.

"Do not be afraid," she said, stooping down close to him, "My name is Agatha Wilson." The man tried to speak, but a look of pain suddenly came into his eyes and he only managed to moan. "Can you tell me your name?" she asked after waiting for his pain to subside.

Finally, he was able to answer her, but his speech was halting and clearly took a great deal of effort. "My name...is Thomas," he whispered. Agatha was happy. At last someone was talking to her! Then she saw that the man had closed his eyes and appeared to be going to sleep.

"Thomas!" she said, urgently, reaching down to shake his arm before remembering that she couldn't do that. "Thomas, you must listen to me!" The man blinked his eyes several times before he was able to see Agatha once again. She could tell by his thoughts that the pain he felt was uppermost in his mind.

"Do I know you?" he asked, clearly forgetting that he had just spoken to her. He looked troubled for a moment before the pain took over again. He began moaning more and an orderly came over to calm him down.

"You must try to sleep," the orderly said to the man. "You bled a lot before we could treat your wounds. You must rest to get better." As Agatha watched, the poor man fell asleep once again. She tried very hard, but she couldn't get him to wake up and listen to her. At first, she allowed her frustration to creep into her voice, but he only grew more restless, he didn't wake up. Remembering the disastrous consequences the last time she lost her temper, Agatha stopped speaking. She stood quietly for a while, watching the sleeping soldier, until she'd managed to calm down.

"I shall find someone else who can talk to me," she thought as she moved on to the next row of beds. As time went on, she was able to make her presence known to the very sick and severely wounded, but their comments about her were not taken seriously. Those tending the young men decided they must be suffering from hallucinations and chose to ignore their insistence that she was in the room with them. "If these men survive, they will probably believe they imagined me," she thought, feeling very discouraged. She had spent several days in the hospital; although she hadn't perceived this passage of time. Agatha realized that she would not get her story told by the wounded men. "I must find the young men I followed here."

As Agatha thought of the Naperville soldiers, she found herself back outside, in the midst of a battlefield. While she'd been trying to talk to the men in the field hospital, the fighting had started. In the chaos, she knew there was no hope of talking to anyone. "I might as well go back to Sarah's graveside. There is nothing I can accomplish here."

As these thoughts were forming in her mind, there was a sudden flurry of gunfire into a group of men near her. Many fell at once, wounded or dead. Several more turned to run, in panic, as they saw that they were about to be overwhelmed, but they ran directly into their own cannon fire and were killed. For the first time, Agatha saw new spirits appear, as the souls of these frightened young men rose above their torn bodies on the battlefield. They were still terrified, unaware that they were dead, and continued to try to seek cover, to escape the enemy. The battle raged on around them and they were convinced that they were part of it.

Setting aside her mission for a moment, she decided to tell the men what had happened to them so they could stop being afraid. "There is no use in running now," Agatha called out to them, "You are already dead." The spirits of the young men turned and looked at Agatha, fear and confusion written on their faces. They looked at each other and then back at her, wondering what a woman was doing in the middle of a battle.

Agatha could read their thoughts and knew they did not believe her. "How long was I dead before I knew it?" she wondered; then she remembered her purpose in being there. "I am wasting my time," she said to herself, "I cannot contact the living here" Saying that, Agatha thought of Sarah and was immediately back by her graveside. But to her surprise, the spirits she had just addressed came with her. They looked around at the unfamiliar territory and then one young man rushed up to Agatha.

"Where are we?" he asked, in great agitation, "Where can we hide?"

"You are dead. I told you that," she said firmly. But the soldier looked at her, unable to comprehend such a thing and shook his head in denial.

"Oh, go hide over there, then," Agatha said in exasperation, pointing to a small grove of trees that still stood a short distance away from Sarah's grave. The men hurried in the direction of the grove as Agatha walked back and forth near the grave, shaking her head. "The only people I can reach are near death, or already dead At least those men will get a Christian burial. They will not be here long." Her thoughts returned to her most important issue. "There must be a way to reach someone living who will listen to what happened to my Sarah. I have not waited alone here to be defeated by death. There must be a way, and I will find it!"

Then, looking once more in the direction of the grove, she watched as the soldiers hid themselves behind the trees. They seemed to be looking around for the enemy and their missing comrades. As she watched, she realized that she could read their thoughts and feel their fear. "Eventually, they will understand what has happened to them, just as I did when I died."

Agatha turned away from the grove and waited for another chance to contact the living. But as she waited, an unsettling thought came to her. "If these men are here with me, and I do not know them, then where is Sarah? This is where she died. Shouldn't she be nearby, near her mother and her grave?"

As Agatha continued to observe her mortal neighbors, she heard them happily discussing the end of the War Between The States and anticipating the safe return of their young friends and neighbors. She also noticed that the soldiers' spirits ran and hid each time a farmer approached the grove of trees where they spent their days. They did not know where they were, they still had not accepted the fact that they were dead, and they feared that each person they saw was the enemy. Their efforts to stay in hiding meant that they couldn't hear the conversations of the Naperville residents and thus did not know that the war was over. Agatha thought that their efforts to keep hidden from people who couldn't see them anyway would be quite funny if they weren't so truly frightened.

Finally, she approached the soldiers in the grove and announced, "The war is over. All the living have gone home. No one can see you. You are dead and cannot be harmed any further." All but the youngest soldier ignored her. He was the young man who had talked to her when they first died. She'd noticed that he had kept one eye on her since they'd followed her from the battlefield.

"Can it be true?" he asked, stepping out from behind a tree and approaching her cautiously. "Can we really all be dead?"

"Yes, of course it is true," said Agatha, relieved that at last someone she spoke to was actually responding to her. "Why do you think no one has seen so many of you trying to hide in one small grove of trees?"

"But how can you see us then?" he asked.

"Because I am dead too," she replied.

The young soldier looked around him, bewildered by this revelation. "Then where are we? Is this Heaven? Could the Devil be playing tricks on us?"

"I do not know where we are," Agatha admitted. "I know that I am able to watch over my daughter's grave and I am trying to make the living hear me, but I am just beginning to learn how to do this. I always believed in Heaven; I thought I would see my mother and my children there when I died."

"I have not thought of my family since the last battle began," said the young man. "I wonder what they are...," Having spoken of his family, the young man disappeared. Then, before Agatha had a chance to return to Sarah's grave, he returned.

"I have seen my family," he said, "but they did not see me. I tried to hug my mother, I whispered in my little sister's ear, but they did not seem to know I was there."

"No one hears me either," said Agatha, nodding her head in sympathy.

The young man didn't hear her comment, he seemed lost in his own painful recollections of the visit he had just made. He continued relating his experience. "They talked about the war being over, how much they missed me, what to prepare for Sunday dinner, and how soon my older sister would be married. Only the cat saw me. I stayed and watched my family go about their chores and go to bed each night. I thought they might hear me when they were sleeping, but they only dreamed about me. They did not hear my words."

"Were you really gone so long?" Agatha asked in surprise, since he seemed to disappear and reappear in an instant.

"I was there long enough to know that I have no place on earth anymore," he replied, sadly. "I can make my family dream about me, perhaps, but...I want to be in Heaven now, the way it was described to us in church." Then, a look of joy came over his face, and he disappeared.

Agatha, who had thought she could never be surprised by anything again, stood stunned by this disappearance. She looked toward the grove of trees where the other soldiers were still hiding, but they were not looking her way. Apparently, they had not seen their fellow soldier leave. Then she began to realize that a great deal of time must have passed since the soldiers were killed in battle.

"Time is not the same for me now," she thought, wondering how long it had been since her own death. "The soldiers must have had a Christian burial by now," she reasoned, "so why are they still here with me, and where did the young soldier..."

Agatha stopped herself, realizing that she might end up following the young man if she thought about him too much. All she knew for sure was that the young man had thought of home, and went there instantly; just as she had been able to return here from the battlefield by thinking about returning to Sarah's graveside. When the young man spoke of Heaven, he disappeared again, looking very happy. But the other men remained. Could it be that a Christian burial was not enough to send the soldiers to God? Could the young soldier have gone to Heaven simply by wanting to go; without a priest's help?

"I have Sarah's soul to think of," she decided, as she forced herself to ignore the young soldier's disappearance. Then she returned to Sarah's grave, and waited.

In the ensuing years, Agatha stayed by Sarah's grave as newcomers built homes and cultivated the land all around her. These were hard-working, practical people, who were not given to noticing the inexplicable. Still, she struggled to make them aware of her predicament.

Agatha learned to 'pick up' objects by using her mind. She'd observed that everything was made up of tiny particles and that if she concentrated on these small particles she could make them change position. With practice, she became very adept at this and was able to move objects so quickly that they would seem to disappear from one place and reappear at another as if in the blink of an eye. She was also able to do this process in a slower fashion that would make an object appear to float in air from one place to another. As she learned to do this, she understood that she was manipulating the molecules of these items. This expression was new to her, yet somehow it made sense. Where this knowledge was coming from, she did not know, but she accepted it gratefully. She knew she must learn everything she could about her new situation if she ever hoped to tell a priest of Sarah's existence.

Agatha practiced these new skills on the settlers. She would move hoes and place her hand on the arm of the person working the land, in an effort to make her presence felt. But the farmers would simply be annoyed at themselves for misplacing their tools or would decide that nearby children were playing tricks on them. Then she decided to try to touch people with her hands.

At first, her hand would just go through the shoulder of the person she was attempting to touch. Gradually she learned to concentrate on keeping that person's molecules in a resistant state so that her hand could touch, but not penetrate, the person's shoulder. This was more difficult than causing an object to change and move. Agatha still hadn't learned how to lay a firm hand on anyone. She realized that her physical touch was not yet strong enough to register on people who had worked hard all their lives. They mistook even her strongest efforts as nothing more than mild muscle spasms and would, at most, massage the area she had touched before continuing on with their work.

Agatha felt more alone than ever. After making so much progress in learning to manipulate objects in the mortal world, she was still unable to get anyone to acknowledge the existence of her spirit.

She waited. The owner of the land, where Sarah lay, died, and a widower bought the property. She hoped that the new owner would be more receptive to her efforts to tell people about Sarah, but he was also an absentee landlord.

By now, Agatha knew she would get nowhere with those who worked the land, so she visited the new owner in his home. He was a well-traveled man, who'd been born in France, and had a love of story telling. His ability to enthrall an audience with tales of his past adventures and some anecdotes about the early settlers of Naperville, reminded Agatha of her life at home in Ireland with her mother. She found herself listening to his tales of his gold mining misadventures in California, and feeling like she was part of the group who had gathered to listen to him. His opinion of the Indians who'd lived in the area was in keeping with her own. He explained that the residents of the Naper Settlement got along well with the Indians because they respected each other's customs. The old man could captivate his audience with stories about the people he knew who were involved in the Black Hawk War and the Mexican War; even though most of his listeners were only old enough to appreciate the excitement and, ultimately, the devastation of the 'War To End All Wars.'

Agatha attempted to reach this man, too. But, when he noticed strange things happening, such as objects disappearing and then reappearing in other places, he assumed old age was playing tricks on him.

Still, she found herself returning to hear him tell his stories. Sitting quietly in a corner of his parlor, she listened, and watched the other guests listening too. Back home as a child, she'd had to remain unseen so that she would not be sent to bed. Now she could pretend that she was unseen for the same reason and forget that she was Left Alone Woman.

The old man died and Agatha sadly waited for a new owner to claim the land. To her joy, a house was finally built near Sarah's grave. Agatha had waited for this day for 90 years.

The house was built for a small family. It had a living room and dining room, as well as a kitchen, bathroom and two bedrooms. There was a basement that could be reached by going down the stairs from the kitchen, at the back of the house. The bathroom and bedrooms were located off a hall next to the dining room. A set of stairs led to an attic that ran the length of the house, and there was a window seat in the attic at the front of the house.

Agatha chose to stay in the attic by the front window, where she could keep an eye on Sarah's grave. The soldiers thought the attic was ideal for them as a hiding place, for they still hid from a nonexistent enemy. Not one to waste her time, Agatha usually ignored the soldiers, but now and again, out of compassion for those poor terrified souls, she would renew her efforts to convince them that the danger had passed.

Meanwhile, though a succession of families moved into the house, Agatha was unable to make contact with any of them. After the house was built, other spirits began to gather there as well. Agatha didn't know who these new souls were, or why they were causing problems, but they used the power of their negative feelings to slam doors, and generally create an atmosphere that frightened those living there.

Mrs. Baker, one of the owners of the house, was a very nervous woman who'd had a great deal of tragedy in her early life. Agatha saw that her attempts to get the attention of anyone in the Baker house had only resulted in increased nervousness on Mrs. Baker's part. Other family members simply were not receptive to her gentle efforts. Agatha waited.

Next came the Whites. This family had lived in the groundskeeper's home at a graveyard early in their marriage. Once Mr. White changed jobs, they had to move, and chose to buy this house. If they had any problems with spirit activity in their new home, they never talked about it.

The Carsons bought the house from Mrs. White after her husband's death. They moved in with their teenagers and Mr. Carson's aunt. Years later, after the aunt died, her footsteps could be heard as she walked around her old bedroom. This activity did not scare the Carsons. They remained here until their family had grown and moved out of the area, then the elder Carsons retired to Florida.

Finally, the Trevors moved in. This couple had many children and Agatha's efforts to contact them were futile. Any noise she made was attributed to one of the children. If she moved objects around, no one noticed. There was simply too much noise and activity for Agatha to successfully reveal herself. Eventually, some of the children were frightened by the sound of the heavy footsteps of a man coming in the back door and going down into a room at the far end of the basement. They were teased by the others for believing in ghosts, and no more was said. In this atmosphere, Agatha realized her efforts to tell them about Sarah were doomed.

Finally, in 1980, the Penrose family moved into the house. They seemed to be more receptive to spirits than previous residents, but at the same time, new spirits were coming into the house. Several of them were disruptive, and became the focus of the family's attention. Agatha didn't know who these spirits were, or why they were causing problems, but they used the power of their negative feelings to slam doors, and generally create a hostile atmosphere that frightened the family.

It was against Agatha's nature to maliciously cause trouble, but she had learned to manipulate her surroundings even more over time. She used her knowledge to move the nutrients in the soil away from the spot on the front lawn where Sarah had been buried. This took a great deal of effort on her part, but she was successful in creating a grassless patch.

The atmosphere in the house grew more threatening, until the family called a psychic to rid the house of the angry spirits. Agatha noticed that, one by one, the newer spirits began to leave the house. Later, even the soldiers left, although she never saw what made them leave. The house grew quieter, and Agatha hoped she would finally be heard. The Penrose family did notice the bald spot on the grass, and their youngest son offered to dig there to see if there was any sign of an old grave that might have created the coffin-shaped spot. His parents wouldn't let him.

Agatha grew more discouraged. But one day, a woman named Pat came to the house to see Sandra. Agatha listened to the conversation between the two women, and realized that Pat was the psychic who had rid the house of the disturbing spirits. If this woman could see, hear, and talk to spirits, then she would hear if Agatha told Sarah's story to her!

Along with some other spirits in the house, Agatha stood before Pat, waiting to be recognized. Pat spoke with each spirit in turn and called upon one of her guides to come forward and lead the way into the light. Agatha listened as Pat explained that souls stayed attached to the mortal world for many reasons: some didn't know they were dead, others were afraid they would go to Hell, and still others were determined to complete some unfinished business on earth.

As she watched Pat release the others, Agatha was finally certain that Sarah's soul was safe. Like the young soldier of years before, who had simply decided to move on, her daughter had also gone on, even though no priest had prayed over her grave. No longer concerned about the safety of Sarah's soul, Agatha turned to the second issue that distressed her. Up to now, no one knew that Sarah had ever existed. All trace of her grave had been swallowed up by the wilderness. If Agatha were to go on now, all evidence of Sarah's existence would be lost forever. Agatha wanted her daughter's life and death acknowledged. When Pat offered to help Agatha go into the light, where she would find her loved ones, she chose to stay, at least for the present. She had waited a long time to tell people about Sarah, and now she would have her chance.

Pat understood that Agatha had a story that she wanted to tell, and suggested that Sandra write it down so it could be kept alive. If Sandra made herself receptive, she said, she could hear what Agatha had to tell her.

Once the writing was begun, Agatha allowed the grass to grow over the bald patch on the front lawn. It had served its purpose.

EPILOG

The day Pat and I discovered Agatha, I sat on the stairs by the window seat and Agatha told me the bare bones of her story. She told me her name, age, that she had come from Ireland, and that she was en route to California as part of a covered wagon expedition when her daughter died. As for her life after Sarah's death, she told me she'd had help from the Indians and I drew the house they'd built her, which I later learned was called a wigwam. In fits and starts over the next several years, I wrote for her. Whenever I thought of all the details needed to complete her story, I would wonder how I'd ever be able to get it written, since, as a Canadian, I knew nothing of U. S. history in the 1800s. The thought of the project, taken as a whole, was overwhelming. I found I had to work on it one small section at a time, and not think about the entire story.

Each week, I would start out with a two or three page outline of a section of her story. My family provided feedback on the content. Using the questions they asked, I would return to the outline and add the detail. When I was on the right track, the words seemed to flow onto the page. But there were times when I couldn't write anything in response to suggestions; I knew then I was trying to write something that hadn't happened to Agatha. For instance, my husband was sure that she must have encountered Joseph Naper, or some members of the Naper Settlement. Agatha hadn't given this information to me, but Bill made a good argument for it, so I sat down to write it. For the next week, I tried to write about such an encounter, but I was unable to put one paragraph together. Finally, I trusted my own feelings and said, "Okay, Agatha, apparently you didn't meet the settlers, so tell me how you avoided them." Then my pen flew across the pages as she described being forewarned of their approach because of their noise, and thus being able to avoid them.

After I'd finished writing about specific periods of time in her life, in detail, I would visit the library and track down information about the place and time I'd described. It was always exciting to discover that nothing I'd written conflicted with the history for the time. In fact, so little is actually written about pioneers in the 1830 time period, that I had to search through a great many books, and use other sources of information, to find the factual confirmation I needed. An example was Agatha's coffee supply. People who read what I was writing told me that she couldn't have had access to real coffee in North America in the 1830s. They suggested that I say she used a coffee substitute, such as chicory. But Agatha had said she had coffee, so I began to look for evidence that coffee had been available in the area at that time. I hunted for this information off and on over the next few months. I could find many textual references to coffee during the 1840s, but nothing earlier. I contacted the sales director of a Chicago-based coffee company and was told that Agatha could have kept coffee for several years in the green bean form if she kept it in a cool, dry place. Unfortunately, he couldn't tell me when coffee had actually become available in North America. Finally, after seeking in all sorts of obscure places, I remembered the *Encyclopedia Britannica*; in it, I read that coffee was first sold in Boston in the 1670s. By the mid 1700s, coffee was available in all the major cities in the colonies. Whenever I wondered if the work came from my own imagination, such confirmations bolstered my belief that I was writing for Agatha. Indeed, I had no difficulty when writing from her point of view. But later, when I started to write my own part of the story, the words did not come as easily.

Over the years, the writing was interrupted several times for legitimate reasons. As with all habits, once I had stopped writing, it was difficult to get started again. When this happened one summer, the small coffin form appeared once again in the front lawn. I returned to the writing, and the coffin disappeared.

As this story has indicated, we have a great many spirits in our house. I have been told by psychics over the years that I attract them. That being the case, I wanted to find out which spirits actually came with the house, and which ones we'd brought. To do this, I interviewed the families and friends of as many of the former inhabitants of the house as I could. I was able to determine that only the spirit in the basement and the one in our bedroom had made their presence felt to previous residents. A former occupant of our house believed that the spirit in our bedroom was that of a female relative. I also discovered that there are other houses in the area that have been, or are now, inhabited by spirits.

I wondered, at first, if we'd brought Agatha from another place, but we found out that there is an area about a third of a mile from our house, near a bend in the DuPage River, where the Potawatomi once camped. That area was later used as a resting place for wagon trains heading further west. When our house was built, arrowheads and crude cutlery were among the items dug up. Therefore, it is probable that Agatha lived and died here.

After researching records on our property, I have been unable to determine if this house was the first structure ever built on the land. I wondered if there might once have been a root cellar to house the food cultivated here by those who'd rented the property. It was an attempt on my part to determine if the unhappy spirit in our basement died from a fall down root cellar stairs on this property or elsewhere.

It had never occurred to me that the Civil War soldier spirits were brought by Agatha, so it was a surprise when I wrote that part of her story. No previous resident of this house had been aware of either Agatha or the soldiers. But they were among the quietest of all the spirits in the house. It wasn't until Pat helped us rid the place of some of the more unhappy souls that Agatha had a chance to make her presence known.

Writing Agatha's story was an important experience for me. It demonstrated that there is a negative side to our strengths. I admired her determination to honor her commitments, in spite of the separations and tragedies that she had to endure. She truly was a woman of strong character. Over time, her determination deteriorated into obsession as she stubbornly refused to seek help from the settlers. Agatha allowed herself to become isolated from society in her single-minded determination to have a priest come to her daughter's grave. But her reasons for staying out of the village were not baseless. From her own experience, she'd have known that new settlers would have little time or resources to share with an outsider. The people would most likely have tried to force her to return to Chicago or New York to seek help. Fearing a negative reaction from the settlers, she'd been reluctant to leave the graveside. Unfortunately, her isolation kept her from learning about the Joliet priest who came to the area on a monthly basis, and could have prayed at Sarah's graveside.

When we allow negative emotions to dictate our behavior, we miss many important opportunities to learn. My fear of the spirits in our home kept me from becoming aware of Agatha for many years. Later, as I wrote about her plight, and felt her frustration and obsession, it became clear that her strong emotions had anchored her to the earth long after she could have joined her daughter. Similarly, the anger of the spirit in the basement, and the fear of Hell felt by the spirit in the main floor bedroom, kept them from moving on. Even the soldiers were stuck here because their fear blinded them to the fact that they'd died. Much has been written about the existence of evil spirits, and I believe they exist, but fortunately they haven't been part of the "other family" in our home.

All of the spirits Pat encountered in our house have gone into the light, except Agatha. In fact, one of the Civil War soldiers has returned, and he's been joined by others from different time periods in U. S. history. These soldiers have been a great help to my son Roger, who was recently in the Army himself. During one of his leaves, when he and his wife and two-year-old son stayed in the upstairs spare room, the soldiers marched around the room, out the door, and up and down the stairs many times. Roger's son could see them and would wave to them each time Roger and his wife heard the soldiers' footsteps moving towards the door. Eventually, Roger took his family downstairs so they could get some sleep. The next day, he told me what had happened before he took his family out for the day. I went into their room and asked the spirits not to bother them again during their visit. "If you have anything to say to Roger, please come to him in his dreams, but don't scare his wife as you did last night." The spirits didn't make any more noise during the rest of Roger's leave, but when he returned to the barracks, they began coming into his dreams to warn him about problems that were developing, in time for Roger to prevent them.

Not long after, I grew concerned because none of us had heard from Roger in a month. He usually was in touch with his wife, at least, on a twice weekly basis. I remembered that Pat had said spirits who go to the light sometimes return to help people, so I decided to put her theory to the test. I went upstairs to our spare bedroom, where the soldiers' spirits stay, and said, "I'm worried about Roger. Please find him and make sure he's okay." I waited to hear from Roger, but I was no longer worried since I noticed that there was none of the characteristic banging on the bedroom door that signaled when one of the kids was in trouble. A week later, Roger called. He'd been out in the field for an extended period. One night, when he was on radio watch, a soldier appeared next to him. From his uniform, and the unfiltered cigarette he held in his lips, Roger guessed him to be of World War II vintage. The soldier looked at my son for a few moments, and then seemed to look through him. Roger looked away for a second, and then realized what he'd seen, but when he looked back, the soldier was gone.

Since Pat cleared the unhappy spirit out of the main floor bedroom, visitors have not had any trouble sleeping there. Indeed, people tend to get very vivid dreams when they sleep in that room, and those dreams offer comfort or solutions to problems they're having.

Now and again, the house will get quite noisy. It usually emanates from the dining room late at night. Doors will slam and footsteps can be heard walking around the main floor. For a while, we would get up in the night and check on the noise, to make sure someone wasn't breaking in. If I was alone in the house, I wasn't really too eager to go downstairs by myself in case there really was an intruder. Our solution was to have a home alarm system put in. That way, if the noise begins in the night, but the alarm doesn't go off, I can relax. It's only the spirits.

When Pat first told me that Agatha wanted me to write her story, I said, "I couldn't. People will never believe it. They'll think I'm crazy." But she encouraged me to try anyway. While researching the story, I've shared our experiences with others. To my surprise, many of the people I've talked to have had their own encounters with the spirit world, or know someone who has. They often have a look of relief on their faces as they begin to share their own stories.

While writing about Agatha's journey, I have come to the realization that strong, negative emotions, such as fear, anger and obsession, can keep us from living our lives to their fullest potential, and from moving on to another level of spiritual development after death. I've used this knowledge to improve my own life. I'm working on expressing my appreciation and affection for people more and am trying not to let fear or worry intrude on my life as it has in the past.

Since seeing so many spirits leave this house and move into the light, Agatha no longer thinks she needs to have a priest for Sarah, but she does want her story told. I sometimes think it's strange that Agatha has not left us to be with her daughter after such a long wait, but then I remember that time is not the same for her. After I finished the first draft of her story, Agatha said that she is staying to help me with something; however, she won't say what that something is. Other psychics have tried to find out why she is staying, but they get the same obscure answer.

I don't know how much longer she will stay with us, but, while telling her story, I have been taken on an exciting spiritual journey of my own. I'm grateful that Agatha shared this with me. She is quiet now, but there are occasional reminders that she's still with us.

One afternoon, when my granddaughters, Tori and Alex, were two and four respectively, they were playing in the upstairs hall. Tori lay on the window seat and Alex came to get a blanket, explaining, "I'm the mother and my little girl is very sick. I need a blanket for her."

"What's your little girl's name?" I asked, amused by their game.

"Sarah," she replied.